FEDERALISM
& POLITICAL
CULTURE

FOREWORD BY
DANIEL J. ELAZAR

FEDERALISM & POLITICAL CULTURE

EDITED BY
DAVID SCHLEICHER &
BRENDON SWEDLOW

Aaron Wildavsky

TRANSACTION PUBLISHERS
NEW BRUNSWICK (U.S.A.) AND LONDON (U.K.)

Library of Congress Catalog Number: 97–16719
ISBN: 1–56000–316–2
Printed in the United States of America

Library of Congress Cataloging-in-Publication Data

Wildavsky, Aaron B.
    Federalism and political culture / Aaron Wildavsky ; edited by David Schleicher and Brendon Swedlow ; with a foreword by Daniel Elazar.
        p.   cm.
    Includes bibliographical references and index.
    ISBN 1–56000–316–2 (alk. paper)
    1. Federal government—United States. 2. Political culture—United States. I. Schleicher, David. II. Swedlow, Brendon. III. Title.
JK325.W46   1997
306.2'0973—dc21   97–16719
                                                                             CIP

Contents

Acknowledgments

Chapter 1 was previously published as the introduction to *The Costs of Federalism*, edited by Robert Golembiewski and Aaron Wildavsky, New Brunswick, N.J.: Transaction Publishers, 1984.

Chapter 2 was previously published as "A Bias Toward Federalism: Confronting the Conventional Wisdom on the Delivery of Governmental Services," in *Publius*, vol. 6, no. 2, Spring 1976, pp. 95–120.

Chapter 3 was previously published in *Society*, vol. 22, no. 6, January/February 1985, pp. 42–49.

Chapter 4 was previously published in *American Federalism: A New Partnership for the Republic*, edited by Robert B. Hawkins, Jr., New Brunswick, N.J.: Transaction Publishers, 1982.

Chapter 5 is a revised and combined version of "A Double Security: Federalism as Competition," *Cato Journal*, vol. 10, no. 1, Spring/Summer 1990, pp. 39–58 and "The 1980s: Monopoly or Competition?" *Intergovernmental Perspective*, vol. 6, no. 3, Summer 1980, pp. 15–18.

Foreword

Aaron Wildavsky was a true federalist. He understood that federalism is about freedom and diversity, that it is noncentralization, not hierarchy and decentralization. He understood that compared to hierarchy, the kind emphasized in modern administration and the organization and governance of administrative states, federalism was on a different continuum and not only had to be understood differently but had to be valued differently, that federalism imposed its own set of values embodied in the norms of noncentralization.

Not only did Aaron Wildavsky believe this, he stated it boldly. He was nothing if not a clear, direct writer and speaker whose message was always presented in such a way as to make at least its principal points easily understood. One assumes that he understood that he was dealing with a world that, because of its preset notions, regularly reinforced from all sides, he, like all true federalists, would have difficulty hearing his message.

Since Aaron Wildavsky's main interest in the study of federalism was to get the principle of noncentralization across, his writings on the subject are generally polemical. He did not hesitate to make his "bias towards federalism" clear and to hammer it home in the best way that he possibly could with his usual humor and elegance, with sharp turns of phrase and insightful analysis.

Aaron's interest in federalism grew from the relatively straightfor-

ward influence of federalism on policy to an intensely normative concern with the promise of federalism and how that promise was being
abandoned in the United States. Federalism, then, was part of Aaron
Wildavsky's game plan. It was not until perhaps fifteen or twenty
years after our first meeting, when Aaron discovered that I and my
colleagues who studied federalism also had a "game," as he put it, and
a game plan, that I began to understand what Aaron was really about.
With his great intellect, diligence, and research skills that seemed
from afar to lead him in many directions, he had a game that he was
pursuing. He was to continue to pursue that game—increasingly focused on political culture, federalism, and the Bible (his game in his
way as it was mine in my way).

Aaron Wildavsky developed his interest in political culture in his
mature years after much research experience. In a real sense, he reached
political culture through Mary Douglas and the Bible. His studies of
political culture, especially his identification of what he sensed was a
critical division between hierarchy and equity, reinforced his belief in
federalism. Preferring equity but recognizing the necessity of combining it with some measure of hierarchy to successfully govern flawed
human beings only strengthened his belief that this synthesis could best
be reached through federalism, both as the best and the most just form of
government in an imperfect world. Given the political cultures of hu-
manity, federalism would not only make the world safe for diversity but
also governable. Yet the self-same human propensities also made the
maintenance of federalism difficult. Hierarchy can very easily triumph
over equity, not because people do not prefer the latter, but because of
the power of those who prefer the former. He saw this story played out
in the Bible and indeed saw this as one of the most profound dimensions
of the Hebrew Scriptures, the great shift in the governance of the
Israelites from Joseph the administrator to Moses the nursing father. He
saw parallel phenomena in the United States in our own time and,
learning from the Bible, he sought to warn Americans.

Aaron and I proceeded to meet often, in Jerusalem or Berkeley, in
Tromso, Norway or Atlanta, wherever in the world we might find
ourselves together in the same city. Not only did our friendship grow
closer, but our agendas began to converge as well around federalism,
political culture, and the Bible, each in our own ways, often agreeing,
sometimes not, but hopefully always with mutual respect.

While, superficially, federalism did not appear to be a central topic in Wildavsky's work, there was very little of his work, at least about American government and politics, that did not touch on it or in which it was not on his mind. For the last several years Aaron Wildavsky had intended to write a book about federalism, and he and I discussed it from time to time. He was distracted from that task by a task that he apparently and correctly considered a prior one, identifying the different forms of political culture that shaped humans as political people and hence were necessary for the understanding of federalism, indeed all politics. We came fairly close to identifying similar political cultural categories. I had come to realize a similar necessity myself and had written about it beginning some years earlier. While we used different terminology, there, too, we were reaching out to the same phenomenon, only to somewhat different aspects of it.

Then, having gotten his political cultural understanding in place, Wildavsky was ready to turn to federalism, when his life was cut short. What we have left are the essays on federalism that he had produced over the latter part of his career. Wildavsky did indeed edit an earlier book on comparative federal systems near the beginning of his career, *American Federalism in Comparative Perspective* (1967), but that was a more conventional collection of articles on how the noted federal systems of our time worked. His later essays dealt with what federalism means, how it should work, and how it was being abused by those in power who protested their commitment to federal principles and practices but acted otherwise. That is the book we have before us here.

In this book, Wildavsky directly attacks the hierarchs and those who would essentially reduce the states to the status of "European prefectures" in the name of "coordination," "rationalization," "efficiency," or "elimination of waste and corruption." As always, Wildavsky calls a spade a spade, naming names and pointing out errors. Most important of all, his critique is a political critique in the fullest sense. He refuses to succumb to the conventional assumptions of public administration when common sense and experience tell us that those assumptions are entirely wrong. To assume rational nonpartisan coordination from the top of a hierarchy flies in the face of all knowledge that we have about government and politics, and Wildavsky says so.

All policymakers and citizens should give heed to his words. Wildavsky suggests that it is precisely because they have not that they have allowed themselves to be misled by the shibboleths of our times that paint pretty pictures and avoid consideration of difficulties, that we are in the fix that we are in. Of course he also recognized that there are those who profit from the present situation, who may indeed understand the truth but who like the results that come from packaging that truth through the myths. Wildavsky pursues this argument in every chapter in this book, perhaps reaching his peak in chapter 2, "A Bias Toward Federalism," in which he cites chapter and verse, pointing out the flaws in a whole range of acceptable works on the administration or implementation of American federalism. His conclusion to that chapter in its last paragraph states it all.

Wildavsky in this respect is an institutionalist, a believer in the power of formal constitutionalized institutions. This comes out most forcefully in chapter 3, "Federalism Means Inequality." He begins that chapter by taking the great students of the American party system and federalism to task for attributing the survival of federalism to the decentralized party system. He advocates a more sophisticated explanation that relies extensively on political culture as he understands it.

As he presents it in chapter 4, Wildavsky's theory of political cultures flows directly from that same policy approach, "How to." He is less concerned with expectations and judgments although he cannot fully ignore either. For this writer, much of what he attributes to political culture is not simply that.

Thus this book offers a good summary of Wildavsky's thoughts on federalism. While Professor Wildavsky dealt with several of the more mundane intergovernmental questions of federalism even earlier, his thoughts about federalism are almost entirely thoughts about American federalism after Lyndon Johnson's Great Society of the 1960s that brought great changes to the American federal system. Apparently Wildavsky's studies of Great Society programs awakened him to the problematics of those programs and others of that ilk, to the maintenance and very survival of true federalism. His response is intelligently polemical, never ignoring the data in his argument, but making his argument on other than empirical grounds.

It may be said that Aaron Wildavsky saw federalism as making the world safe for diversity. Like Wildavsky, this writer views that as a noble end and a major dimension of federalism. Indeed, Wildavsky became even more concerned about the ultimate meaning of federalism as he became more concerned with political culture, perhaps because he discovered inequity among the political cultural forms that he identified. As a democrat he tried to minimize the influence of hierarchy and maximize that of equity, which led him in the case of the United States at least to a strong commitment to federalism and from there to his polemic against what was happening to federalism in the contemporary United States.

The chapters in this book more or less trace the progress of his thought along those lines as he moved first to the argument that true federalism is noncentralization, then to federalism as competition, and then combining both for the reassertion that real federalism is possible only in a confederation. He stops short of stating that the United States should have remained one. While he does not explicitly say that, it is clear from chapter 6 that he had come to that conclusion when his pen was so sadly and prematurely stopped.

Aaron Wildavsky's conclusions should give us pause. For someone who began as a nationalist with a minimally critical, if not uncritical, acceptance of the American federal system as it was in the 1950s and whose work in that decade and in the 1960s concentrated on how the system worked, a task that he performed so brilliantly, the shift in his thought should give not only partisans of federalism but partisans of the United States and American liberty considerable food for thought.

In the last analysis, Wildavsky's writing on federalism was not only polemical but utopian, uncharacteristic of most of his other works. It is as if federalism became a touchstone of belief for him in that he saw successful democratic politics as the politics of federalism. Hence, in many respects he painted a brilliant but oversimple picture, not recognizing in his writings what I know that he recognized in his empirical understanding, all of the eddys and currents that made American federalism too complex to be described as unidimensional in the way these writings, taken alone, might lead the reader to believe.

For Aaron Wildavsky, writing after the 1960s, cooperative federalism had already become coercive federalism, and only competitive federalism, the introduction of market principles into relations between the federal government and the states, could provide the benefits that federalism was designed to provide. Like many converts to capitalism, at times he seems to attribute a much greater capability of the market to deal with complex problems than experience tells us is the case. That, in essence, is the utopian dimension of Wildavsky's federalism.

The limits of what we have from Professor Wildavsky's pen on federalism is that most of it was put on paper in the fifteen years following his awakening to the question of federalism and thus is not far enough into the post-1960s to note the revival of state energy and its implications, the persistence of the activist United States Supreme Court and its implications, and the rise of federal mandates and its implications. Taken separately or together, none of the three contradict Wildavsky's writings, but they would have nuanced those writings in both directions in various important, if sometimes subtle, ways. It is for that reason that his utopianism at times seems, to one who has immersed himself in the field, somewhat simplistic, something that Aaron Wildavsky definitely was not. Much of that appearance is eliminated in chapter 6 wherein Wildavsky contrasts the American confederation with the subsequent American federation to make his case for noncentralization.

What can we learn from all of this? Aaron Wildavsky wrote to teach, to guide, and to provoke, so that we can learn. If this was generally true, it can be said to have been especially true in his writings about American federalism. He sought to save the American federal system in order to save American liberty. That is why he wrote polemically and why his recommendations have a utopian quality about them.

At the very least we must consider the fact that Wildavsky wrote as he did about federalism, that if such a person as Aaron Wildavsky, so sober and realistic a student of the political process and public policy, appreciated federalism in the way that he did and wrote about it and its tribulations in the way that he did, we must pay serious attention to the matter. We must understand his understanding of federalism and consider its validity. Most especially, we must understand his conclusion that the American federal system has to be brought back closer to its confederal roots if it is to remain federal.

Aaron Wildavsky was my kind of federalist. Although to the casual outside reader it would look at times as if we were disagreeing with one another, in fact it was probably at those times that we were most in agreement and I cannot think of any major point about federalism on which Aaron and I disagreed. The differences between us were, as far as I could see, two. One, my interest in the study of federalism mostly has been analytic while his was polemical, and my study of federalism has been from the outside in while his was from the inside out. That is to say, as in all his studies he looked at the problems of federalism from a policy point of view. What will it do? How will it do it? What will be the consequences of what it does and the way it does them? His polemics were policy polemics—"If you will do so, you will get this"—whereas I have defined my task as the understanding of systems.

This book is not Aaron Wildavsky's complete word on the subject of federalism. For that, one has to read through most of his ouevre, beginning with his early forays into the issue of community power and on through his last studies of the Bible and political culture. This book is, however, his considered thought on the subject of American federalism. He leaves that as a legacy for us to which an increasing number of his students and colleagues are taking heed. I know that he would want that number to grow in the hope that telling the truth to power in the case of federalism will bear fruit.

Editors' Preface

This is the second title in a series of Aaron Wildavsky's collected writings published posthumously by Transaction.[1] Nevertheless, Aaron selected and arranged the six chapters found here before he died of lung cancer in September 1993. All that is missing from this collection is a never-initiated piece on American federalism in the 1990s, which he intended to co-author with David Schleicher, who, like Brendon Swedlow, was one of his research assistants.

Versions of all but the last essay appearing here have previously appeared elsewhere. Consequently, most of this volume tracks the published pieces fairly closely. However, chapters 3 and 4 of the draft Wildavsky left behind were significantly different from the published versions. Chapter 3 seemed to have been partially, but not completely, revised because the designation "egalitarian" had been substituted for "sectarian," an earlier usage, while the writing was less polished than that of the published version. We reconciled these differences by using the published version's stylistic improvements. For Chapter 4, the differences were more substantive than stylistic, so that we could not tell if the manuscript chapter was an earlier or later version than the published one. We decided to preserve this variation by reproducing the manuscript version here.[2]

Attentive, front-to-back readers of this volume will discover several passages in several essays which are almost identical, but, we decided, are not redundant since they serve different purposes in the places where they appear. Nor, we think readers will agree, are they paraphraseable, for in these passages Aaron-the-pastry-chef serves up federalism as various tasty cakes—layered, marbled, fruity. His personal favorite, as will become apparent, is federalism conceived as a birthday cake, since such cakes are crafted to promote the happiness of the individuals receiving them rather than the administrative needs of a distance bakeocracy. At an rate, Aaron believed that if something was worth saying once, it was worth saying several times, and if this a useful precept anywhere, it is certainly one here.

With the exception of chapter 2, all of this manuscript was written since the late 1970s when culture became a very important explanatory variable for Wildavsky. Consequently, these essays strive to say something about the relationship between political culture and federal structure. However, as Daniel Elazar rightly notes in his foreword, the essays found here tend to be more polemical than analytical, an observation Martha Derthick also made while on a 1994 American Political Science Association (APSA) panel honoring Aaron's contributions. The kind of culture Wildavsky favored and the kind of federalism he felt would best promote the individualistic way of life are very visible in these writings. Yet the "grid-group" theory he adopted from British anthropologist Mary Douglas and shaped into his cultural theory was not simply an ideological battering ram, as his many analytical uses of culture in other essays in the other volumes of his collected papers attest.

As an editor of these other papers and as a student of Wildavsky's cultural ideas, Swedlow in particular hopes that students of federalism will look beyond Wildavsky's preference-infused presentation to the analytical potential of the theory and its concepts. Professor Derthick recommended as much in her APSA remarks:

> There are rich possibilities in seeking to link Aaron's cultural theories of political regimes with the actual functioning of American federalism. If one wishes to assess the state of play among the competing political cultures in this country—hierarchy, competitive individualism, egalitarian sectarianism—there is no more revealing place to look than the condition of American federalism. Correspondingly, if one wishes to assess the condition of American federalism, there may be no better tool than the cultural theory he devoted a decade of the crowning years of his career to developing."

Derthick calls chapter 3 "the most challenging and analytic of the essays," saying "Students of federalism should, in my view, pick up where this highly tantalizing and suggestive article leaves off."

We would also encourage the theoretically minded student of federalism to use chapter 3 as a stepping-stone to a more analytic use of Wildavsky's cultural theory. Moreover, the study of federalism provides a unique opportunity to refine and further specify the characteristics and dynamics of the theory's cultures. Professor Elazar's much more intensive and extensive studies of federalism have been accompanied by the description and explanatory use of subcultural types that are very similar to those developed by Douglas and Wildavsky.[3] Aaron and one of his students, Richard Ellis, compared and attempted to reconcile the relatively minor differences between these types and their accompanying concepts.[4] These efforts could also form a basis for more rigorous attempts to define and measure the presence of different cultural types, which in turn should allow less fuzzy and more empirically informed specifications of the relationship between political culture and federal structure.

Aaron retained a spirited interest in federalism in his finalweeks. In one of Schleicher's last conversations with him, he spoke excitedly from his hospital bed on the subject that dominated that summer's political landscape: Yes, health care reform was needed —but the reform should be led by the states! A variety of approaches could be tried, tailored to local circumstances; the smaller scale of experiments would limit the cost of mistakes; successes could be emulated. How, he wondered, could the superiority of the federalist approach over national scale reform not be obvious?

***

A great many people helped get the extended version of Aaron's basic "bias toward federalism" into print. Gail Sydow retyped the published pieces, incorporating the changes Aaron made that we described above. His colleagues at Berkeley's Survey Research Center, Professors Henry Brady and Percy Tannenbaum, took turns supervising our editorial efforts. Irving Louis Horowitz, Transaction president and a longtime friend of Aaron's, guided us from afar. We were supported, to various degrees and at various times, by grants from the Bradley and Smith Richardson Foundations. Aaron Wildavsky held the Class of 1940 Chair in Political Science and Public Policy at Berkeley, which also underwrote our editorial work, as did the Survey Research Center. Doris Patton, his long-serving administrative assistant, incorporated our changes to chapter 3 and put all notes in a

common format. Mary Wildavsky participated as necessary to keep
things moving along. Hopefully both she and Aaron will find in our
efforts the discharge of some small part of our great indebtedness to
him—for ideas, opportunities, friendship, and our shared interest in
environmental science.

David Schleicher
Berkeley, California

Brendon Swedlow
Richmond, California

Notes

1. The first is *Culture and Social Theory* (1997), edited by Sun-Ki Chai and Brendon
   Swedlow, with a foreword by Charles Lockhart and Richard M. Coughlin.
   Craftways (1989, 1993) should be consulted for Aaron's intentions regarding the
   series.
2. Chapter 1 is substantively a slimmer version of its published counterpart, but here
   most of the differences can be traced to Aaron's editing out those passages that
   delved too deeply into the chapters in the edited volume to which this essay was
   an introduction. Chapter 5 merges two earlier pieces by cutting about half the
   material out of the original "Federalism as Competition." Finally, chapters 2 and 6
   are almost exact reprints of their previously published versions.
3. See Daniel J. Elazar, *American Federalism: A View from the States*, 3rd ed., (New
   York: Harper and Row), 1984; *The American Mosaic: The Impact of Space, Time,
   and Culture on American Politics*, (Boulder, Co.: Westview), 1994; and *Cities of
   the Prarie Revisited: The Closing of the Metropolitan Frontier*, (Lincoln: University of Nebraska Press), 1986. A collection of studies testing and refining Professor Elazar's subcultural ideas can be found in John Kincaid, editor, *Political
   Culture, Public Policy, and the American State* (Philadelphia: Institute for the
   Study of Human Issues, 1982).
4. See Michael Thompson, Richard Ellis, and Aaron Wildavsky, "American Political
   Subcultures," chapter 13 in *Cultural Theory*, (Boulder, Co.: Westview), 1990; and
   Richard Ellis, "The Subcultures of Daniel Elazar: Individualism, Traditionalism,
   and Moralism," pp. 165–169 in *American Political Cultures*, (Oxford: Oxford
   University Press), 1993.

1

E Pluribus Unum:
Plurality, Diversity, Variety, and Modesty

Sometimes simplicity is a virtue, sometimes it is a curse. In the study of federalism it has become a curse. We take it as axiomatic that every mode of social organization has its contradictions and that none is satisfactory under all circumstances. Following Aristotle, there has been a search for mixed regimes, hopefully combining the best and avoiding the worst. Thus federalism has been proposed as a combination of opposing principles, centralization and noncentralization, both hopefully locked in a creative tension. Yet the proliferation of names of the motley crew of resulting forms should give us pause. Maybe there are more than two ways to organize life and more than a few composite regimes that come about from mixing them up.

Virtually all the modern study of organizations is concerned with bureaucracy. The hierarchy, with its nest of inverted Chinese boxes, its specialization and division of labor, its inculcation of the sacrifice of the parts for the whole, has been virtually the only form to receive serious consideration. Noncentralization, or self-organizing systems, based on spontaneous rearrangements among independent entities, comes in belatedly by virtue of contrast. Thus political regimes are either centralized and hierarchical or noncentralized and competitive. Is there, then, nothing in between? There is the egalitarian regime, sometimes called "collegiums" or "clans." Egalitarian organizations are characterized by a purely voluntary form of organization in which members are roughly equal in resources as well as in decision-making ability. Mixing the three—centralization, noncentralization, and equality—leads to more variety than current conceptions allow.

Centralization via hierarchy is one answer to the problem of social order; the people involved are to live together by accepting structured inequality, a place for everyone and everyone in his/her place. Its advantages lie in the subordination of individual egoism to the collective community. Pomp may belong to the higher orders but lower strata also get protection because they are recognized as belonging to the same collective. Evils range from dictatorship, to stultification, to inability to recognize or learn from mistakes. The mitigating cure is often called "decentralization"—a delegation of authority on a regional or functional basis. This increases local efficiency at the cost of lengthening the distance between the central authorities and those closer to the conditions and people affected. The evil of noncentralization is either lack of community, resulting in dependence on hierarchy for maintaining and altering the rules governing transactions, or unbridled competition, leaving those without entry fees to drop out. The resulting inequalities create strains in the social fabric. The evils of egalitarianism are both a lack of authority, which leads to interminable delay, and rampant envy over small differences, which leads to perpetual splits and an inability to tolerate factional competition, leading to endless charges of conspiracy for bringing inegalitarian measures into a purported community of equals.

What happens when these forms coexist and interpenetrate one another? Whether we talk about political democracy, scientific activity, or economic growth—all these crucial aspects of modernization are based on competition. Democracy is often conceived of as competition for office, science as competition over ideas, and economic growth as competition for resources. Some of the curse is taken off centralization by placing hierarchies in competition with one another, whether in elections, markets, or striving for fame. Some of the curse is taken from markets by hedging them about with restrictions, limiting freedom of contract, and establishing a social minimum. And some of the onus is taken from egalitarianism by limiting the amount of redistribution, adhering to criteria of merit, and maintaining economic growth, which permits rewards to increase even if inequality is not significantly diminished. The uneasy combination of organizational forms, this armed truce between rival visions of the good life, is encapsulated in the American romance with federalism: *E pluribus unum*.

We all agree that federalism is good, which helps us agree to disagree over exactly what it is, so that different political regimes can continue to coexist. The costs of federalism, conceived not merely as a division of legal responsibility for governmental functions but as the diverse organizational elements of modern pluralist democracy (pluralism standing for a combination of organizational forms), are the costs of this delicate balancing act, so delicate that at no one time or under no set of conditions can it possibly be satisfactory to the adherents of its constituent elements.

A Plurality of Conceptions

What are the costs of federalism? "The price of more pluralism," Nelson Polsby writes, "is a less orderly political life." The price is paid in terms of contradiction:

> What individualists cannot choose, of course, is a society in which they retain the right to move about as they like or need, exercising their options to change their jobs, marital status, geographic location, names, hair, lifestyles, political commitments, while others hold still and provide them with the comforting support systems—stable neighborhoods, lifelong friendships, personalized and unbureaucratic professional services—of a more stable, confining, and less resourceful age.[1]

Parties decline in favor of the media, and trust in leaders and institutions depreciates in favor of individual choice. Apparently we cannot have unfettered personal expressiveness and a stable collective life. Put that way, put pungently, so we cannot avoid the contradiction, Americans are indeed getting what they want even if, looking at the collective consequences of individual choices, these are not always (or often) what the very same people think they need.

Every regime, Theodore Lowi tells us, ultimately creates a politics consonant with itself. That is why, seeing contemporary politics triangulated rather than bifurcated, he foresees the probability of a three-party system, with one of the parties a socialist party with a social-democratic program. If it hasn't happened yet, the new party may be just around the corner. Why, he asks, has there been no strong socialist party in America's past? Because, he answers, pointing to the paltry constitutional powers given to and exercised by the national government until the 1930s, "with the state governments as the course of legitimation for . . . capitalism . . . there was simply no common political experience that would lend much plausibility to a socialist analysis of American society or a socialist critique of American capitalism."[2] Why is there, then, an enhanced probability of a party dedicated to socialism today? His answer is that "the expansion and strengthening of a national state . . . is the one condition conducive to the emergence of a *bona fide* socialism in the United States."[3] It is not society that creates a socialist regime in Lowi's causal connection, but the enlarged state that creates the conditions for socialism.

Observe that where Polsby stresses social changes affecting political structure, Lowi views the policy reversal of the federal government and the states ("federalism in economic matters has all but disappeared" and "national government policies were fairly frequently antagonistic to capitalism") as affecting political structure.[4] This is another example of the Schattschneider-Lowi doctrine that policy causes politics and vice versa.[5]

If Polsby's piece can be taken to exemplify the argument of political sociology, and Lowi's constitutional approach the argument for political structure, my essay is an attempt to add political culture —the shared values legitimating desired social relations that make up the plural political forces in the United States.[6] The division of power between levels of government is dependent not only on geographic separation fortified by constitutional representation but also on social differences. A person living in the same town or neighborhood most of his life, for instance, might be motivated to climb the party ladder to a position of prominence. The same person who keeps changing residence (as Jo Freeman pointed out to me) might be better off attaching herself to a national interest group, available whenever she wants and willing to recognize prior participation no matter where it occurred. The major political parties, especially the Democratic party, have been able to accommodate and to an extent co-opt the new interest groups in time-honored fashion. More recently the Republican party has opened up to (some would say been "taken over by") Protestant fundamentalists. Where, then, might social democracy, if not socialism, the former less interested in nationalization of industry than the latter, come from? According to my calculus of political regimes, centralization, bringing with it the strong national government social democracy requires, constitutes a commitment to hierarchy, a commitment far from the pluralist forces of self-expression Polsby identifies. Social democracy could come (and undoubtedly does stem) from a belief in greater equality of result, a belief not too far removed from other ways of diminishing differences among people visible nowadays—sexual freedom, gender equality, challenges to expertise, reduction of regionalism.

If the main impulse leading toward social democracy is a desire for purely voluntary social relationships, with mutual consent required anew in each and every transaction, an anomaly may be explained and a deeper difficulty revealed. The anomaly is the coexistence of demands on government for redistribution with a withdrawal of authority from the very same bureaucracy that has to make good the promises.[7] The desire for equal outcomes may well lead to demands for government to share incomes, while the desire for voluntary association may simultaneously lead to resistance to the coercion involved in doing that very thing. The deep difficulty referred to is that social democracy has a chance to thrive when its main instrument—governmental action—is regarded as a positive good. Authority and responsibility remain within hailing distance. But a form of socialism that distrusts hierarchical authority—that is, the very kind on which it is most dependent—is likely to self-destruct. Self-organizing federalism is impossible without a semblance of a center. Centralization without a center is a contradiction in terms.

A Diversity of Practices

"Nearly everything has become intergovernmental." With these words Donald Kettl sums up the current state of affairs, for in our time "it has become far more difficult to differentiate national, state, and local functions."[8] Along the way, participation in making and implementing policy by all sorts of private interests and levels of government has markedly increased. The prior specialization by level of government has been superseded by specialization according to program. The theme has been expansion—of federal funds, programs, issue networks, models of delivery, judicial involvement, and concern over the concomitant diffusion of responsibility. Distributive politics in Congress, Kettl concludes, has been rivaled both by administrative rule-making and by judicial determination of what the substance of the policy is really supposed to be, a determination often guided by different notions of equality. Meanwhile, a good deal of actual service delivery has been contracted out to private providers, adding further to the number and kind of stakeholders in the federal system.

There is no doubt that the federal system has proved adaptable. But the cost of adaptability has been a decline in accountability. "Such a system," Kettl warns, "makes it difficult to determine just who is responsible for a problem at hand or how it can be resolved. Furthermore, it makes it impossible for anyone to tackle the problems of the system as a whole."[9] Coordination has been sacrificed for responsiveness.

So what? To those who seek centralization and the maintenance of hierarchical differences specifying the correct division of labor, the federal "mishmash" is a nightmare. If everyone is in charge somewhere, someplace, sometime, then no one center of authority is in charge all the time. I take it that, according to the framers of the Constitution, that is the way it is supposed to be. But the Constitution is, of course, silent on how fragmented relationships within and among policies are supposed to be.

It might be thought that extreme fragmentation would be sufficiently like a market to satisfy supporters of noncentralization. Not really. There is a political market for programs but it is hardly unfettered. Thus adherents of competitive individualism have sought to replace categorical grants, stipulating what is to be done, with block grants giving states and localities greater latitude. So long as the states are playing with other people's money, however, rather than asking what they are prepared to give up in taxes to get what they want in services (a good is worth what one has to give up to get it), so long as the doctrine of opportunity costs does not apply, markets are being administered and there can be no genuine state and local consumer sovereignty. Transferring taxing powers to states would suit the market mentality better than passing costs on to taxpayers in other jurisdictions.

Egalitarians are in a quandary: the more centralized programs become and the narrower their focus, the greater the likelihood that funds will be targeted toward those most in need. Here they join with centralizers in urging that the parts of the federal system sacrifice for the whole by redistributing income. Thus egalitarians press for categorical grants and judicial intervention to raise the rate of redistribution. They want expenditures per pupil to be uniform across the United States. By the same token, homogenizing outcomes decreases diversity, thus decreasing responsiveness to locally determined needs. Here egalitarians would ally with noncentralizers. If small is not always beautiful to them, at least it is not as ugly as large-scale domination.

Much the same is true of noncentralization and equal results. All ends are partially but not wholly achieved. Viewed one way, this is a trite conclusion, merely restating the pattern of a mixed system with which we are all familiar. Viewed another way, we have an answer to an important political question: how come nearly everyone is dissatisfied with the current condition of the federal system? Given the expanded size of programs, there is more centralization, noncentralization, and equal distribution than before. That is just it; since no set of political preferences has been entirely satisfied, yet none has lost out entirely, partisans of each are dissatisfied. But the one thing they can agree on is that the result is a "crazy-quilt pattern" which some call federal, in which there is no complete victor but many incomplete winners.

Let medical policy stand as a paradigm of delivering a vital service under a federal system, with guidance from Carolyn Tuohy and Robert Evans, who focus on a Canadian province.[10] Everything that is wanted is there—numerous private providers, layers of governmental bodies, complex financial arrangements, conflict within and between the stakeholders, considerable accomplishment, and no end of criticism. Certainly the system is viable: it works. Canadians and Americans enjoy among the highest standards of medical care and, without being perfect, there is considerable equity: with variations, rich and poor, black and white, city dweller and country resident see doctors and stay in hospitals about the same amount of time with much the same results. The health care system is also vulnerable: inflation in medical costs runs two to three times the national average in the United States. The causes are well known: the public and private dollars pouring into the system swamp available resources, bidding up the price, more so in the United States because there are more sources of subsidy. But the same principle applies in Canada as well. Incentives for cost containment are weak and, as Tuohy and Evans explain, we also know why that happens. Few individuals pay the cost of care or even know what it is; units of government pass costs upward. The organizations that spend do not pay; those who pay do not plan; and those who plan do not have the resources. Whenever there is a fixed financial limit, costs decline, but that is fiercely resisted on grounds of equality or access to or quality of care. Why, then, does Canada have less medical inflation than the United States? The answer is that the Canadians rule out all sources of spending other than governmental and, to accommodate that limit, ration access to hospitals and expensive procedures, the overflow going to American hospitals.

James Fesler's precept—"decentralization . . . is constrained by the need to adapt to or modify the relative centralization/decentralization of related administrative functions and of the broader political and economic context"—is true.[11] But the context is so overwhelming—in the United States medical care is financed by tax deductions (now partially limited), untaxed "fringe" benefits in the form of comprehensive company plans, Medicaid for the poor, Medicare for the elderly, veteran's benefits, and some actual individual payments —that the total bill is hardly affected by state and local arrangements. This is an exaggeration; benefits do vary by state and country. But in the aggregate the general conclusion is valid. The degree of areal decentralization may matter administratively by channeling local demands, as Tuohy and Evans show, but this hardly affects the cost of service and, except for small variations, its quality as well.

Perhaps we need a new principle: money swamps interdependencies. Another way of saying the same thing is to affirm Tuohy and Evans's observation, no doubt of interest to a professor who taught us most of what we know about public administration, to wit: "The most striking feature of the health care industry is its absence of management."[12] Why manage when someone else is paying the bills?

Well, now, is health care centralized, noncentralized, or what? The only plausible answer, apparently, is "all of the above and then some." As Tuohy and Evans put it:

> Providers are subject to regulation, restriction, financial constraint, and a wide variety of administrative harassments revolving around funding levels. But the line decisions about how care shall be provided to particular patients, and what mix of personnel and equipment shall be used in its provision, are decentralized to a degree that must be unique in economic organization. Despite large centralized payment mechanisms and huge hospital centers, health care remains a cottage industry. Providers are responsible for individual patients; but if the aggregate performance of the delivery system is inadequate . . . there exists no accountable management. Nobody is responsible for health.[13]

Why does this state of affairs continue? Because, our perspicacious observers continue, "the existing organization of delivery creates an incentive structure that penalizes a provider at any level who tries to be more efficient."[14] There is the telltale phrase —"Nobody is responsible at any level"—that answers the question about whether federalism matters in health care.

Suppose, however, that our only concern was to limit costs, leaving quality and access as secondary considerations, though this is certainly a counterfactual supposition. If private practice and private insurance were forbidden, centralization funded by a single national appropriation would cost less. This is so because both spending and taxing to support it would come to the center for decision, as it does in Britain, leading to trade-offs against other valued national purposes. Complete decentralization, allowing only private fees for service and eliminating all subsidy, would also be a lot less expensive: doctors and hospitals would be constrained by what potential patients could afford. It is a mixed system—private and public payments, with spending spigots at numerous levels of government—that is most expensive. Pluralism pays more.

Now if we relax our rigid criterion by admitting other important criteria back into consideration, the compromises between cost, quality, and access return the discussion to its starting point. Higher costs go along with greater responsiveness.

Among the conundrums of centralization versus decentralization, none is hoarier, more common, or more in need of sage advice than the extent of and conditions under which delegation of power is appropriate. Delegation has a cultural context. It depends in part, as all human arrangements must, on the personalities of those involved, but in largest measure it depends on congruities in values and the pattern of social relations they justify. As the scope of government grows, delegation becomes ever more essential. If doubts about authority rise even faster, however, delegation is bound to become problematic, either a rationale for blaming subordinates or a means of attacking the integrity of superiors.

If we ask what sort of regime facilitates delegation, we immediately turn to the centralized hierarchy. An egalitarian regime, by contrast, cannot delegate because no one has the authority to set out the terms of discretion. Noncentralized organizations delegate for specific tasks, removing authority when the job is done. Not only Rome but early American states delegated extreme power to generals, but only for limited periods.

It all adds up this this: American political cultures are made up of people who organize to accept, reject, and limit delegation. Differences over the extent and conditions of delegation, therefore, are empirical questions about what works well; disputes about the desirability of delegation at all reflect divergence of values over whether the political system within which delegation is to be practiced deserves our trust.

A Variety of Winners and Losers

Unanticipated consequences are a staple of life. False consciousness is an existential state, if by that is meant that things do not often turn out as we wish. The federal principle is a good example. Choosing centralization, or equalization, or noncentralization, may depend in part on allegiance to the principles themselves, but the choice also depends on our estimates of the consequences. Given the vast variety of interactions within a federal system, fortified by a large array of programs and participants, uncertainty about outcome is integral to the enterprise. Among the many things about which the stakeholders must be uncertain is what level of government, as well as which organizational arrangements, will leave them and those they care about better off compared to alternatives. The switch of political forces in America from states' rights to national sovereignty and back again depends on which arenas are perceived to advantage and disadvantage stakeholders at particular times and in regard to specific issues. A new Supreme Court member or two, for example, might make recourse to that arena more or less advisable. Advocacy of state supremacy might seem less advisable to Republicans if they keep losing out in contests for state houses but win the presidential office more often than not. The struggle over the federal principle is full of surprises, not the least of which involves winning the principle only to lose the substance.

Herbert Alexander continues the theme of winners and losers.[15] It is not easy to say whether and in which respects the phenomenal growth of political action committees (PACs) to support candidates for office in the United States represents gains or losses either for one or another federal principle or for those who favor or oppose them. PACs began to strengthen labor union political activity, which still continues. But as an unanticipated consequence of imposing financial limits on individual contributions to candidates, PACs proliferated among business and then a diversity of other single-issue interests. The difference is that whereas the "fat cats" of old were generally satisfied with social contacts and access to support broad preferences, the new PACs are both better informed on how to exert influence and more dedicated to specialized concerns.

There can be little doubt that the effectiveness of states and localities in the national policy process depends in significant measure on the strength of political parties, a capacity critically dependent on their (and their candidates') ability to raise money. Social life affects political practice. As Alexander observes:

> American politics is shifting from neighborhood precincts to socioeconomic bases representing a common occupation or ideology. Political Action Committees (PACs) are better able to adapt to these changing bases than are political parties, because PACs can focus on single issues or give priority to emerging issues and still survive with limited constituencies, whereas parties must be more broadly based in order to thrive.[16]

Since Alexander believes not enough money is spent on elections, he wants to increase the flow from all sources—national party committees, individual contributors, and PACs—by removing existing restrictions on fundraising. He would also like to strengthen parties as conduits for campaign cash. The larger the role party organizations play, the more candidates will be beholden to them and the less to funding sources with specialized interests. Alexander argues that "the new single-issue ideological and PAC constituencies are as much in need of mediating political institutions as the old ethnic constituencies."[17] It may be that it is not the division of powers between governmental institutions that matters most, then, but the ability of government per se to act so as to integrate the diverse forces in American society. In a country where the federal system is often used as a synonym for government, the failure of federalism would signify the collapse of government itself.

The proportion of local government revenue provided by the federal government rose from 2.6 percent (2.8 percent for municipalities) in 1960 to 16.3 percent (22.8 percent for municipalities) in 1980. The federal contribution increased seven to ten times in two decades, a sea change if there ever was one. Dependence on federal financing must be far greater in certain cities.

Was this good or bad for federalism? Assuming that "he who pays the piper calls the tune," a downward trend would be regrettable for centralizers and an upward trend unfortunate for noncentralizers. From the perspective of egalitarians, assuming the bulk of funds went from richer taxpayers to poorer municipalities, the reduction that occurred during the 1980s is extremely unfortunate. Only adherents of a market model of federalism (viz. President Reagan) can point with pride, though the decline in dependence is not nearly enough to suit them.

Were a significant number of cities to grow in reliance on federal funds to a point approaching half or more, the question would arise as to whether the local level, adding in state support as well, could be said to retain independence. And without local independence, a federal system can hardly be said to exist.

Modest Proposals

What should government do, if anything, about "reindustrialization"? If help is needed, what level of government should give it? Whenever intractable problems appear, decentralization seems attractive, if not as a present solution, then as a way to learn about future solutions, if not as a cure, then as a way to diffuse public retribution over the disease.

"Policy," Garry Brewer informs us, "generally resolves to difficult problems of institutional design and organizational modification much more than simple decision-making routines."[18] Thus it comes as no surprise to learn that questions of federal structure constitute an important part of the discussion. The problem, as Brewer sees it, is not how to get government to do more or less but to do whatever is done more efficiently. One objective is how to put an end to things that do not deserve to be continued. The harsh name for that is "termination." Experience tells Brewer that new public investments should have "self-destruct" mechanisms to prevent them from becoming new obstacles to termination. In the end, following American tradition, he recommends dispersing the difficulties:

> Transference is particularly important if one takes seriously the threats to social order a possible legitimacy crisis holds. Put another, starker, way: It is far safer for local, state, and private authorities to take credit or blame for direct operations than it is to continue taking careless risks with the consensus that binds the nation together. . . . The approach also diffuses blame in the inevitable cases where operations fail or are contentious. Were, for example, a reconstituted RFC [Reconstruction Finance Corporation] to fail, blame would fall immediately on national authorities, but were a municipal assistance corporation in Pittsburgh to falter, damage to the total social order would be negligible by comparison.[19]

Even (or especially) when questions defy answers, there is always one thing to be done, for the federal principle is always available as a solution looking for a problem.

Enough of piddling with minor changes. Enough of asking the old questions: Which level of government should handle what policy? Are states or the national government closer to the people? Is there too much or too little national government? Are the states capable of exercising whatever functions they perform? Robert Golembiewski proposes to sidestep all these questions.

When his friends feared being singled out for the wrath of Dr. Johnson in responding to a petition, they made it circular and signed it "we the circumscribers." So, too, Golembiewski has circumvented both the old praise and the new complaints about the federal system by proposing to design it on a new basis.

Truly it is federalism, to the extent federalism must have an areal basis, with a vengeance. No more (at least no more large) departments on a functional, meaning here a programmatic, basis. Instead the domestic activities of the national government would be organized on an areal basis. There would be a competitive federalism but the competition would be between geographic areas, whether states or some other entities.

Golembiewski's slogan is straightforward: Area should dominate. The emphasis is on integrated delivery of services to citizens. Responsibility is for reaching targets of service—housing, income, literacy. "The essence of the alternative model," he sums up, "is a balance at the highest organizational levels—the centralization of policy and oversight, and the decentralization of implementation—with the key facilitator being the enhanced ability to measure performance."[20] The role of Congress and the president would be to "[set] policy boundaries for any exchanges between areas, and in monitoring these exchanges."[21] Golembiewski's "policy bias" is stated succinctly:

> Exchanges should be as little fettered as possible. This not only is consistent with American political philosophy but also implies a convenient management tool. Freedom of exchange would aid in monitoring performance in the several areas, for example, as people vote "with their feet."[22]

Considerable program variance between areas would be encouraged. By establishing the principle of "unity of purpose" rather than "unity of command," Golembiewski hopes that interaction among areas, under competitive conditions, with a minimum of guidance, would work better than the traditional model.

The American people might like to exchange their present discontents for a new set—government by areal administration, as fundamental a challenge to the existing administrative order as has been mounted in recent times—that certainly has the virtue of being different. Adherents of centralization might welcome the opportunity to escape putting the blame on bureaucracy. And if positions at the national level appeared paltry by comparison to the bad old days, there would be many more at the areal level. If centralization requires large national hierarchies, they would be big losers. But if with a smaller center came opportunities for greater guidance, they might be mollified. Advocates of noncentralization would find Golembiewski's federalism more to their liking, provided that the national government did not set social minimums too high or preempt too much of the country's financial resources. (Evidently, taxing and spending would have to be higher at the areal and lower at the national level than they are today.) For the very same reasons, proponents of an egalitarian regime would have serious doubts. Their noncentralist, "small-is-beautiful" wing might be content with seeking the good (read self-sufficient, small-scale, and egalitarian) life at the areal level. Their struggle would then be devoted to converting each area to their lifestyle. They would win in some areas, we might expect, and lose in others. But angered at inequality, they might seek support from centralizers to raise social minimums closer to maximums. Small central bureaucracies would suit them, provided they enforced egalitarian outcomes.

All this is hypothetical—but with a purpose. The existing federal system contains elements of centralization (policies controlled by the national government), decentralization (programs delegated to field offices and/or states and cities), and noncentralization (policies controlled by states and local units). What a mess! What confusion! No one can figure out a consistent set of principles to rationalize who does what to whom. Too true.

But now we have an inkling as to why this convoluted state of affairs exists. Convoluted but not necessarily irrational. Existing arrangements are politically rational, not because they are perfect or cannot be improved, but because they accurately reflect the mixture of political preferences in this country.

Notes

1. Nelson Polsby, "Prospects for Pluralism in the American Federal System: Trends in Unofficial Public-Sector Intermediation," in Robert Golembiewski and Aaron Wildavsky, eds., *The Costs of Federalism* (New Brunswick, N.J.: Transaction Publishers, 1984), pp. 21–36, at 31–32.
2. Theodore J. Lowi, "Why Is There No Socialism in the United States? A Federal Analysis," in Golembiewski and Wildavsky, eds., *Costs of Federalism*, pp. 37–54, at p. 49.
3. Ibid., p. 52.
4. Ibid., pp. 50, 49.
5. Elmer E. Schattschneider, *The Semi-Sovereign People* (Hinsdale, Ill.: Dryden, 1975); and Theodore J. Lowi, "American Business, Public Policy, Case Studies, and Political Theory," *World Politics*, 16 (1964): 676–715. See also Aaron Wildavsky, "Policy as Its Own Cause," in *Speaking Truth to Power* (Boston: Little, Brown, 1975).
6. "Federalism Means Inequality: Political Geometry, Political Sociology, and Political Culture," in Golembiewski and Wildavsky, eds., *Costs of Federalism,* pp. 55–72
7. See Aaron Wildavsky, "The Three Cultures: Explaining Anomalies in the American Welfare State," *Public Interest* (Fall 1982): 45–58.
8. Donald F. Kettl, "The Maturing of American Federalism," in Golembiewski and Wildavsky, eds., *Costs of Federalism*, pp. 73–88, at 73.
9. Ibid., p. 86.
10. Carolyn J. Tuohy and Robert G. Evans, "Pushing on a String: The Decentralization of Health Planning in Ontario," in Golembiewski and Wildavsky, eds., *Costs of Federalism*, pp. 89–116.
11. Ibid., p. 89.
12. Ibid., pp. 99–100.
13. Ibid., p. 100.
14. Ibid.
15. Herbert E. Alexander, "Political Parties and the Dollar: After the Reforms," in Golembiewski and Wildavsky, eds., *Costs of Federalism*, pp. 165–186.
16. Ibid., p. 165.
17. Ibid., p. 183.
18. Garry D. Brewer, "Industrial Policy: Disinvestment, Retrenchment, and the Evolving Role of Public and Private Institutions," in Golembiewski and Wildavsky, eds., *Costs of Federalism*, pp. 205–236, at 206.
19. Ibid., pp. 230–231.
20. Robert T. Golembiewski, "Organizing Public Work, Round Three: Toward a New Balance between Political Agendas and Management Perspectives," in Golembiewski and Wildavsky, eds., *Costs of Federalism*, pp. 237–270, at 259.
21. Ibid., pp. 261–262.
22. Ibid., p. 262.

2

A Bias Toward Federalism

There is no way of escaping the grand question: where do we want the balance between national and state power to be drawn in regard to which issues? Under a national regime, states and localities carry out national instructions; the problem is how to improve their obedience. In a federal regime, states and localities are disobedient. The operational meaning of federalism is found in the degree to which the constituent units disagree about what should be done, who should do it, and how it should be carried out. In a word, federalism is about conflict. Federalism is also about cooperation, that is, the terms and conditions under which conflict is limited. A federal regime, therefore, cannot be coordinated any more than it can be controlled or coerced. Federalism requires mutuality, not command, multiple rather than single causation, a sharing instead of a monopoly of power. One can only determine if the federal beast is alive by whether it kicks. How and whom it kicks, and whether it gets kicked back, should be the subject of an organization theory of units in a federal system.

Federal principles ought not be limited to relations between national and state governments. If it is good for power to be divided and shared, that principle must also prevail in relationships among states, and their cities, counties, and special districts. Let us call this principle—under most conditions a larger number of smaller units will deliver services better than a smaller number of larger units—the federal bias. It is not an unalterable bias; circumstances do alter cases. It is, however, a bias. In the absence of evidence to the contrary the federal principle should prevail. Where evidence is lacking or inconclusive, which is most of the time, faith in federalism requires this bias. The burden of proof, for those who share this bias toward federalism, must be on people who propose that bigger and fewer is almost always better.

The promotion of economic development is a "classic" function of government, one that has long been acceptable in many quarters and that antedates contemporary conventional wisdom about the planning and organization of government for serving the public. In the recent past, the federal government has experimented with several ways to promote economic development, particularly in the country's less developed areas—most recently through the Economic Development Administration. Those experiments have given rise to a literature which poses the questions as to how this particular governmental service should be provided in a federal system. This essay will be largely concerned with the theoretical issues raised by organized action to advance practical economic prospects in a federal system. The research covered and the issues examined, I believe, are broadly representative of the current wisdom on federalism and the delivery of governmental services.

No one writes on a clean slate. Research does not ordinarily emerge out of a void; it is based on common understandings built up over decades by other toilers in the same vineyards. Whether the assumptions are explicit or implicit, they guide new authors along old paths. The bulk of the relevant research falls within two opposing traditions in the study of economic planning and political federalism. On the economic side, long-range comprehensive planning is ranged against short-term, piecemeal adjustment; on the political side, concentration of power is posed against its dispersal. The political economy of one uses bureaucratic metaphors—hierarchy, coordination, consistency— while the other makes use of markets—competition, conflict, bargaining. To make a market analogy good in the political arena requires numerous participants who bargain to increase mutual advantage. The bureaucratic image necessitates as few units with as little conflict as possible. While markets are designed to clear any number of antagonistic interests, bureaucracies depend on a few agencies operating in the context of agreed objectives. For purposes of exposition, I shall refer to one as the cooperative-coercive and the other as the conflict-consent model. The normative prescriptions of the two models can be summarized as follows: where conflict is viewed as functional, consent is considered essential. Where cooperation is normative, coercion is deemed legitimate. Because units should cooperate, they ought to be coerced when they conflict. When units ought to differ, they can only resolve their differences by consent.

The Cooperative-Coercive Model

In "Organizing for State and Multi-State Development Planning," William T. Goodman offers a good statement of the cooperative-coercive model. His major contention is that "modern administrative requirements for area development cannot be met by the old order, in which each plane of government either fights its battles in a sovereign and isolated way or is frustrated in attempting to carry out a program in conjunction with other units. Cities and states have for too long engaged in a profitless conflict which neither side can expect to win . . . because of the rigid system in which they are caught up."[1] The assumptions are clear: the old order of innumerable sovereign units of government engaged in profitless conflict is counterproductive and must go.

One answer is planning. Goodman recognizes that little meaningful planning occurs and that most of it is based on ad hoc response to immediate needs. He believes that planning would lead to certain benefits, such as "securing a more rational and efficient set of major planning and development organizations," "alleviating the intense disharmonies posed by major metropolitan complexes," "restoring the vitality of minor civil divisions," "recognizing and mediating conflicts over jurisdiction and competition for investment and resources within a single economic and social region," and "reducing the bureaucracy inevitably associated with centralized control."[2]

How would planning accomplish these purposes? The answer is cooperation through planning: " [A] new spirit must infuse the state to produce results. . . . The states or their regional organizations must begin to work together."[3] Goodman sees four primary responsibilities for state planning: review of local and regional planning, development of the state economy, a comprehensive plan for physical growth, and a review of capital projects. All of these necessitate coordination.

Goodman's discussion of that elusive term is sharp and to the point:

> Coordination ... requires a hierarchy of units wherein the coordinator exercises
> supremacy and, at least, tacit coercion against units lower in the hierarchy. The
> power to coordinate places a club over the head of those who are to be coordi-
> nated. The dilemma therefore is this: coordination will tend to founder when
> exercised by the planning agency against operating departments, if planning itself
> is set up as an operating department.[4]

If coordination is a synonym for coercion, how will planners acquire
the necessary power to impose their will? What, in their search for
power, will prevent planners from taking on the coloration of the
operating departments who live from day to day? "To date," Goodman
writes, "there has been more concern by planners for being 'where the
action is,' often at the expense of their fundamental raison d'être,
comprehensive planning."[5]

One might easily be accused of creating a straw man of comprehen-
siveness in planning if Carlisle P. Runge's and W. L. Church's "New
Direction in Regionalism: A Case Study of Intergovernmental Relations in Northwestern Wisconsin" did not already exist. "Our review,"
these authors begin, "has led us to conclude that there is an unfortunate lack of coordination of efforts [on] all [planes] of government and
that the programs involved would be more effective if governmental
procedures required a higher degree of interagency and intergovernmental cooperation."[6] After describing northern Wisconsin and men-
tioning some hundred federal and state departments involved—"The
list of agencies seems endless" —they note that under Office of Management and Budget Circular number A-95 a notification and review
system has been established so that federal projects may be viewed in
advance by state, regional, and metropolitan clearinghouse units. To
them "it seems certain that at the very least, a much increased level of
state and regional planning will be induced and a higher degree of
regional program consistency will be achieved."[7] Why this should
happen, whose interest it is to make this happen, is never discussed,
which may explain why what seemed certain to them has not yet
occurred.

Runge and Church believe that further coordination will not be
fully achieved unless a local planning unit has "at least some degree of
control over such investment, and unless it has some minimal capacity
to enforce its recommended priorities within the guidelines of comprehensive plans."[8] What role would there be, then, for states or for the
federal government? "It is too much to expect," the authors are aware,

"that local planning agencies will ever be allotted sufficient power actually to direct affirmatively the local expenditures of state and federal funds, and with good reason. . . . But it is not too much to suggest that such local agencies, if they are indeed sufficiently supported to be able to attract competent staff, be granted a minimum negative authority to reject proposals which are found to be seriously inconsistent with comprehensive area plans."[9] How, then, will conflicts be resolved among planes of government? Will federal and state agencies provide funds to areas that thwart their own plans? The authors place their trust in a worthy trinity: faith, hope, and charity.

Their basic idea is that power should be concentrated on each plane. There should be a single economic development agency on the local, county, multicounty, multistate, and federal planes.

> We believe serious attention should be given to developing a series of multi-state-federal regional groupings that would encompass all of the states. . . . We propose . . . that each Regional Council be headed by a coordinator who is a deputy to the President, rather than a chairman from one of the functional agencies. To be sure, this would constitute a significant delegation of Presidential powers, but this executive presence in the field is exactly what is required if decentralization of authority is to be manageable and effective.[10]

What happens if a cabinet member objects to what the president's field representatives are doing? How does the president handle conflict between his field representatives and governors or mayors or congressmen? Runge and Church suggest that the power of governors would be enhanced, but they do not say how or at whose expense. They do say: "One can hope that the Regional Councils could secure a firm enough relationship with the Senators and Representatives from the respective regions to allay their concern, and that to the extent this could not be achieved, the elected representatives would be willing to forego their traditional direct influences over federal programs in their home states in recognition of the breadth and complexity of administering shared federalism."[11] Here we have it all: faith that interests and objectives are similar; hope for a voluntary renunciation of power; charity toward other planes of government without expecting a return in the form of change in policy.

Picking up where Carlyle and Runge left off, one of the important modern works on federalism, *Making Federalism Work: A Study of Program Coordination at the Community Level* by James L. Sundquist (with the collaboration of David W. Davis), states that efforts to make the federal system work better by providing "planners, coordinators, expediters, facilitators, communicators" have given us "a more complicated federal system—one with five, six, or even seven [planes] of government where three or four sufficed before."[12] How, they ask, should the federal system be organized to accommodate the new neighborhood structures and multicounty organizations? They believe that "A coordinated approach to intergovernmental relations requires the introduction of a new force [on] the regional [plane]—a supradepartmental official with responsibility and authority to speak for the federal government as a whole in matters of intergovernmental relations. In the absence of such a spokesman, there will not be a satisfactory channel of central communication between the federal government as a whole and state and local governments."[13] These coordinators would not control substantive programs but would be in charge of managing, overseeing, and coordinating—which may or not be the same thing.

Aware that congressmen and cabinet members might resist presidential agents who would exert authority over the departmental personnel or who might become political rivals, the authors feel

> It would be essential that the appointees to the regional positions not be politicians or even public figures. Their primary interest would have to be not in the substance of particular policies but in administrative systems—specifically, systems of intergovernmental relations. . . . The regional representatives would represent the President not in his roles as party leader and policy advocate but only in his role as chief administrator.[14]

The paradox is that presidential agents without partisan backing would be useless, and with it they would become the enemies of every existing official.

The authors must be convinced that the president would gain something from their suggestions because they insist that "guidance, however, can come from but a single source of authority—the president. It is he who must apply the principles and the doctrine in proposing legislation to the Congress and in directing the execution of the laws."[15] But would presidents welcome becoming directly involved in every conceivable local quarrel? Present trends are directly away from overt federal involvement in localities. Through "enterprise zones" presidents would get a little credit and none of the blame for disappointed seekers after federal largesse.

What role are the states supposed to play in this picture? Sundquist and Davis suggest "a differential approach to federal-state relations,"[16] by which they mean taking into account the considerable variation in the competence of state governments.

> Given this diversity, the advantages of state participation can be maximized and the disadvantages minimized only if the federal government can adopt a *differential* approach, working through some states and bypassing others in the same programs. To make such an approach possible, federal-state relations have to be converted from a *legal* concept, in which the states collectively negotiate in the legislative and administrative process for rights and powers that all of them then possess, to an *administrative* concept, in which the federal government exercises judgment as to how much reliance can be placed on each state and reaches an individual understanding with that state governing federal-state relationships.[17]

American states would thereby be reduced to European prefectures.

There is, in the authors' view, a place for coercive action by state governments. They are to compel various local jurisdictions to fall in with comprehensive model cities plans. "If the model cities coordination process is to succeed," the authors assert, "state agencies will have to be directed by their governors and legislatures to enter without reservation into that process and to conform their programs to the model cities plans, and it will require state leadership—and perhaps coercion at times—to bring counties, school districts, and other independent governmental bodies into that process also."[18] The role of states, apparently, is to enforce federal programs on recalcitrant localities.

And the localities? It is all for them. "The central premise," the authors state, "is that the effectiveness of the execution of federal programs depends crucially upon the competence of community institutions to plan, initiate, and coordinate. The federal contribution of money and ideas and leadership to community programs is indispensable, but it is still only a contribution. . . . No amount of review by, and coordination among, federal agencies is a satisfactory substitute for what must be done properly in the first place within the community itself."[19] Communities, apparently, must be forced to be free.

What is the proper role, then, for the federal government? Sundquist and Davis say that

> What remains for the federal government is to reconcile its competing strategies and settle upon a unified approach to perfecting the design of the community-

[plane] machinery, getting it established, and then supporting its coordinating efforts. To attain that unified approach to community-[plane] coordination by all of the agencies of the federal government working in concert is the heart of the problem of coordination [on] the Washington [plane] of federal assistance programs.[20]

Why haven't these programs worked well in the past? Because they "are left to the sponsorship of individual federal agencies." Sundquist and Davis argue:

> The facts of bureaucratic life are that no Cabinet department has ever been able to act effectively, for long, as a central coordinator of other departments of equal rank that are its competitors for authority and funds. Nor does coordination spring readily from the mutual adjustment of Cabinet-level equals within the federal hierarchy. It must be induced, overseen, managed, and directed from the supra-Cabinet level—in other words, from the Executive Office of the President, where the authority exists to identify problems that need settlement, expedite discussion, referee disputes, make binding decisions, and issue orders. Voluntary bargaining among Cabinet departments of equal rank is no substitute for a decision-making structure led by a presidential staff officer who carries the authority and the governmentwide perspective of the President. . . .
>
> Somewhere in the Executive Office must be centered a concern for the structure of federalism—a responsibility for guiding the evolution of the whole system of federal-state-local relations, viewed for the first time as a *single* system.[21]

Let us pursue the rationale of this position before we stop to consider its implications.

Another name for a presidential agent is secretary of a department. If department secretaries are supposed not only to support the president but also be responsive to the interests entrusted to their care, then these relationships would necessarily reemerge within the new structures of presidential agents. Whereas cabinet members sometimes have a certain authority and political influence, however, these presidential agents would have neither. Neutrality can be neuter, a polite way of referring to impotence. It might look on paper as if the president were running the whole country, but it would be even less true than it is now.

The authors complain that "it makes little sense for the federal government to encourage the communities to construct elaborate coordinating systems that the federal government's own agencies are then left free, individually and collectively, to ignore."[22] Cities complain about interminable delays and about inability to get their plans funded when they have worked so hard to submit them. True, the authors point out, "the federal agencies cannot be bound absolutely by whatever the local planning process comes up with. They must guard not only against waste and extravagance but against proposals that may distribute the benefits of federal programs unfairly or in other ways inconsistent with the national purpose."[23] The feds, in their view, must be the guardians against proposals by one community that might adversely affect others, or that might cost more than the federal government felt it could afford. They continue:

> Yet it is one thing for federal officials to draw the line against a local proposal on grounds of illegality, waste, inequity, discrimination, spillover effects, or unavailability of funds and quite another for them to substitute their judgment for that of local communities on matters that do not involve these considerations. Our field interview notes are filled with assertions by local officials that federal decisions are being made on matters that should be wholly within the competence of the communities.[24]

Naturally, no federal agency would ever substitute its judgment for that of a locality; it just happens that all these other reasons—illegality, waste, and so on—are good ones for turning down or altering what the localities wish to do.

After this, it comes as some surprise to read that "yet the principle of decentralization is sound." Local decisions "are *potentially* better than those made [on] the national [plane], because only [on] the community [plane] can the community be seen whole, only there can all the community programs be interrelated, only there can the systems of comprehensive planning and program coordination be established and operated, and only there can widespread citizen participation be organized and the contributions of the citizens blended with those of the professionals in the decision-making process."[25] Only there, apparently, does perfect liberty consist of the right to agree with the grant federal coordinator.

In case of disagreements, who should prevail? The final word of Sundquist and Davis is that "*as the machinery begins to measure up to its promise and gains in competence,* the conscious policy of the federal government as a whole—and, hopefully, the state governments as well—should be *to defer increasingly to local judgments.*"[26] A marked tendency by President Clinton's first term is his deference to states that want to try something different.

On the national plane, according to Robert Warren, despite lip service to the contrary, elected Federal decision-makers have, on numerous occasions, clearly rejected a policy of granting subnational entities the power needed to control the range of socio-economic phenomena necessary for economic development programs or for effectively coordinating the activities of Federal agencies within a specified territorial area. An agency can be charged with the responsibility for coordination, planning or development without being delegated the requisite authority or resources to perform these functions. Consequently, officials of regional bodies tend to be in the position of claiming to achieve goals for which they are statutorily responsible but for which they have no formal power to accomplish.[27]

Of course, if any government had it all, it would be unitary, not federal. But why is there so large a gap between rhetoric and reality?

One answer emerges from Robert Warren and Geoffrey Wandesford-Smith's "Federal-State Development Planning: The Federal Field Committee for Development Planning in Alaska." Its goal was to supply the "most effective use of Federal and State programs and funds for advancing the long-range progress of the State."[28] To do this the FFC was designated "the principal instrumentality for developing coordinated plans for federal programs which contribute to economic and resources development in Alaska."[29]

The authors point out that the establishment of the FFC really constitutes a sort of prediction that the organizational arrangements embodying it will lead to the desired results. Though the underlying assumptions do not exist in a codified form, the authors dig them out. First is that the federal agencies "will cooperate among themselves to establish a comprehensive plan and then coordinate their programs in light of it."[30] Second is that the feds will have adequate authority to respond to regional circumstances despite the national policies of a department or bureau. Third is that the state and localities in Alaska will be able to unify themselves and commit themselves to participate with the federal entities. But regional bodies lacked authority and interagency rivalry was the norm. "A review of the history of Federal, Territorial and State governmental activities in Alaska . . .," the authors find, "indicates that the characteristic behavior of public entities failed to provide any evidence that the conditions outlined above existed or could be established easily."[31] Why?

The problem appears to have been that Congress wanted coercion in the abstract but conflict in the concrete. It wanted to give new powers to an area-wide body so long as it did not have to take old ones away from the functional federal departments. The FFC did not so much result in contradiction as embody these opposing impulses—let rival camps contend. Congress' substantive theory was based on the cooperative-coercive model but its procedural theory was dependent on conflict and consent.

The Conflict-Consent Model

A division of power would not normally be thought of as good in and of itself but as a means to desired ends—peace, prosperity, domestic tranquility. Sharing powers on a geographic basis has been defended as aiding national defense,[32] diffusing by dividing domestic conflict,[33] and facilitating innovation (e.g., the states as laboratories).[34] The test of federal theory is federal action—superior delivery of services.

Evidently two measures are required, one of excellence in delivery of services (the dependent variable) and the other of governmental structure (the independent variable). Now experience teaches us that objectives of governmental programs tend to be multiple (because we want many different things), conflicting (because we as a people want incompatible things like conservation and use of natural resources), and vague (because ambiguity hides differences and facilitates action). Nevertheless, it is sometimes possible to get agreement on such measures of local services as reading ability of children and adults' chances of getting mugged. The seemingly insuperable obstacle comes from an inability to get agreement on the definition of federal structure. What kind of division or sharing of powers, on paper or in practice, to what degree, in regard to which objects, must a government possess to qualify as federal in structure? No answer will be forthcoming here.[35] Instead, keeping delivery of services firmly in mind as the end in view, I shall concentrate on two structural attributes—size and number—without which no claim of federal superiority in delivery could be made.

If it were true that the smaller the number of units and the larger the size of each one, the more effective the delivery of services, it would be hard to conceive of an effective argument for a federal structure. The more unitary the state, the more effective it would be. Field offices might be feasible but state and local governments would be gratuitous. Within loose limits, the larger the number of units, and the smaller the size, the pro-federal argument must go, the more effective the delivery of services. To argue the reverse—bigger and fewer is better—is to reject federalism.

According to Sperlich's law—all interesting relationships are curvilinear—there must be sizes so small or so large as to render the units ineffective. The federal argument must be that beyond minimum size—a few thousand or tens of thousands of people—all useful division of labor and specialization can be achieved. There must also be numbers of units too large to be effective but the case for the federal principle must be that so large a number is hard to conceive, running, say, into the tens or hundreds of thousands.

Naturally, there are trade-offs between size and number. From the federal viewpoint, the curse is taken off size by number: the larger the number of units involved, the larger each unit can be without decreasing effective delivery of services. The value of size, then, depends on number: the smaller the number of units, the more large size contributes to ineffective delivery of services.

The division and sharing of powers between a single federal and various state governments is only one (and not necessarily the best) test of the efficacy of the federal principle. It is difficult to arrange tests of federal principles, since the number of states is usually just a handful, rarely exceeding the fifty of the United States of America. Fortunately, there are hundreds of counties, thousands of cities, and even larger numbers of special purpose (water, sewer, school, fire, irrigation, etc.) districts whose operations involve variations in both number and size in the delivery of services. These endlessly proliferating units live by conflict and cooperation. They conflict because each is out to make the best deal it can for itself. They cooperate so long as their arrangements suit each other better than any available alternative.

In "An Operational Approach to an Efficient Federal System, Part I, On the Specification of Horizontal Relationships," Eugene Smolensky, Richard Burton, and Nicolaus Tideman set out to determine the degree to which problems in metropolitan areas are due to defects in governmental structures.[36] In so doing, they could learn whether actions should be geared to meeting the problem directly or should be "designed to compensate for the awkward federal structure of the government." Rather than examine a set of individual problems, which they say would be "little more than an exercise in taxonomy," they chose the course of proceeding theoretically by setting down in a quite abstract way the general conditions for the design of a spatially dimensional federal system which would not give rise to that class of problems generated by the present organizational structure of the government.[37]

Informed with these principles, planners could then specifically identify problem areas which would therefore "be more effectively open to
straightforward solution."[38] The ultimate objective was to provide "the
EDA with a design for an optimal federal system which may be used
as an analytic tool or guideline for evaluating the performance of the
existing system and its structural components."[39] That way public ser-
vants could tell whether too much or too little is being spent on public
goods and whether the boundaries of the polity are congruent with
those of the problem.

"It may fairly be said," they begin, "that the present areal jurisdiction of our multi-[plane] governmental units have been established by
tradition and modified by expedience, rather than by the guidelines
issuing from any widely recognized theory of governmental boundaries. In consequence, governments and their citizenry come together
under circumstances in which the legally defined spatial boundaries
are increasingly out of alignment with the boundaries of the substantive policy issues on which they interact."[40] This, at least, is the understanding upon which the conventional wisdom of reform is based.

The guiding theorem they use is: "If the optimal production level
for a public good is to be achieved, the spatial extent of the political
domain in which the output decision is to be made must embrace all
those upon whom taxes or other non-user costs are to be levied as well
as all those who will benefit from that output. Thus, one (remedial)
solution to inefficiency in the provision of public goods caused by
geographical spillovers is to create a new [plane] of government which,
in effect, forces congruency between the boundaries of a political unit
and the boundaries of a spatial area affected by that political unit."[41]

Using a series of stringent assumptions, Smolensky, Burton, and
Tideman conclude that "the most efficient prototype . . . has a size and
market area that maximize average net benefits per households
served."[42] Among the assumptions made are the following: "Our analysis implies known benefits," "the demands of all households are equal,"
a "uniform plane," and "perfect information."[43] Obviously, none of
these conditions has been or is ever likely to be met.

The authors observe that a competitive solution could not guarantee
that the districts would fill their uniform plane completely because it
would take time for districts to reshuffle themselves when the gaps
appeared:

But in the meantime, there would be investment in the wrong places, which would have to be written off before the shifts could take place. In order to avoid this misplaced investment, a solution that considered the whole plane in the first step would be needed. That is, a planner would be needed to carve up the plane into equal-sized adjoining districts of the optimal size for the provision of the good. The households in each district would provide themselves with a facility of the optimal size, in a location consistent with a pattern in the plane, and no investment would be wasted. Thus the price of efficiency in our uniform plane is a greater concentration of power.[44]

Several times the authors emphasize that "We neither expect nor recommend that government policies be undertaken to exactly achieve the ideal result and, of necessity, an important class of urban problems would continue to remain in any case."[45] They also say that to the extent that EDA is interested in the distribution of income it may wish to alter the policy implications.

The hierarchical bias is evident. Achieving efficiency within the boundaries of the plane demands that the federal government decide who will perform what functions in which geographic locations. Persuading local units to abolish themselves is no mean task. Short of that, what incentives might be provided local development units to act in ways federal officials deem appropriate?

Stephen Cohen's idea, in "Planning in Essex [County, New York]: An Analysis of the Current EDA Approach to Planning in Rural Areas, and Some Suggestions for Reforms," is to understand how the incentives are now structured in order to change them later. Starting

with an outline of a typical plan, with its discussion of the demographic characteristics of the area's unemployment and its inevitable list of projects, Cohen points out that it is the same everywhere. The reason is, "They are planning for the same things according to the same rules."[46] Their purpose is to get money from the feds and they produce a plan because otherwise EDA will not pay them. The locals are willing and even hopeful that they will learn something from planning, but the plan is a secondary and not a primary product. Thus the plan becomes a document designed to sell the feds on pet local projects. There is no consistency here in the sense that a sewage project can be part of economic development in one place, health in another, and agriculture in a third. In order to produce the projects, locals need outside consultants who know what EDA wants. What the consultant does is get the census, make up the tables, and send them to EDA. "In exchange for its planning money, the EDA more often than not gets the census read back to it in the rasping voice of an itinerant peddler of canned plans."[47]

Cohen declares,

> Our object is to refocus local efforts away from the preparation of planning docu-
> ments (which are seen as the price to pay for keeping the office going and for
> getting specific "projects" funded) and on to the serious business of planning—
> affecting local behavior. At present the planning document is seen as the end of
> planning (in both the sense of the goal and the place where activity stops)
> . . . . The way to do this is to change the cueing system of information and incen-
> tives that has shaped rational actions by a large number of actors into a basically
> irrational charade called "planning." One way to begin this process is to reallocate
> tasks between the center (EDA) and the local agencies, to create a new division of
> labor in order to change the output.[48]

Cohen's first major suggestion is that the EDA get the census information and send that to the localities instead of the other way around.
Should the EDA try to make more creative use of this information so
that it will pose more challenging questions? This will not save the
EDA much money; it might even cost more, Cohen believes, but it
would free up talent in the local areas to work on more creative things.
Since all data are leading, "The point is to change the direction in
which it leads. The present . . . data leads the local agency straight to
filling in the blanks on the standard OEDP."[49]

Cohen's analysis helps by showing federal officials they are offering the wrong incentives on their own terms, which is not to say that
locals would necessarily be made better off by a different set. Pierre
Clavel, in "The Politics of Planning: The Case of Non-Metropolitan
Regions," cries out, "there seem to be more ideologies channeling the
attention of multicounty agencies to state and federal [planes] than
there are ideologies directing their attention locally."[50] The coopera-
tion-coercion model, based on assumed congruence of interests within
a framework of comprehensive planning, allows only one correct answer, not many.

Will no one step forward to champion local interests by helping
them on their own terms? Samuel M. Leadley, author of "Organizational Innovation: Case Study in Planning and Development"[51] comes
to the rescue by setting up a process model of institutional change. He
investigated the formation of multi-county organizations to determine
the factors that were related to their success. Then he stated the conditions influencing change. (1) "The uncertainty of the relative advantage of the innovation." Local influentials were concerned about the
applicability of general ideas to their counties.[52] (2) "The success of
the initial applications of the innovation." Early success generates a

willingness to go further.[53] (3) "The presence of enabling state and federal legislation" which leads to (4) "The availability of extra-regional financial assistance." Money makes the world go round.[54] (5) "The level of competition for the performance of governmental services." The presence of many actors, even if they don't exercise their authority, leads local groups to fear erosion of their power.[55] (6) "The lack of internal resources to provide the basic investment necessary to achieve the minimal standards of performance of necessary services." If local groups already had the resources they needed, they would not be so tempted by federal funds.[56] (7) "The increase in local definition of need to perform certain services." Locals act when aspiration outruns achievement.[57] (8) "The degree of divisibility of the innovation." This characteristic permits organizations to exist on very modest budgets and to engage in numerous trials.[58] (9) "The choice of neutral names for the new regional organization." This helps by suggesting lack of threat.[59] (10) "The degree of local experience in performing the service for which the new multi-county organization was to assume responsibility." The more they have to begin with, Merton's famous "Mathew effect," the more they will get.[60]

Donning the mantle of strategist, Leadley advises promoters of local development to: (1) begin with the services for which the participating units have prior experience; (2) select from these services the one that has the most immediate prospect for pay-off and the least new direct local expense; (3) help local groups in meeting their most immodiate needs even if other use of resources would appear to have longer-run high priority; (4) consider sacrificing staffing efficiencies in the interest of more dispersed location; (5) exploit initial success in order to decrease the uncertainty of leaders about the advantages of new organizational forms; (6) "At all points in time . . . enter local systems through local influentials or leaders rather than bypassing them because of their potential opposition to the adoption of the innovation. Access to these influentials is best found through involvement of resident representatives of extra-local systems."[61] Pick those people, in other words, who have already shown interest and activity. The best thing about this advice is that it deals with the motivations of the actors, so one can believe there is a modest chance that reasonable men might behave in the desired way. The implications of dealing with existing elites for reinforcing whatever structure of power exists in local communities should also be recognized.

The most deeply ingrained assumption in all the literature on the relationship between governmental structure and policy outcomes is that rural and urban problems are traceable to the large number of overlapping jurisdictions, governments, and special authorities that exist in America. The most critical issue in organization theory for area development, in my opinion, concerns conflict-consensus versus cooperative-coercive models of organization. Are externalities to be taken into account by internalizing them in ever-larger organizations to coerce cooperation, or through facilitating a "crazy-quilt" pattern as a multitude of conflicting interests bargain out their differences in the mixed-motive game we call the political process? Which alternative generates the most information on preferences? Imposes fewer costs? Inculcates the most dynamism? Leads to integrative solutions?

Warren and Wandesford-Smith state this issue:

> The assumption that the efficiency and responsiveness of government in an urban area decreases as the number of jurisdictions increases is open to serious question in relation to metropolitan areas. Even stronger issue can be taken with the proposition in terms of the effect of a very small number of local governments for development purposes. It can be argued that the existence of [a large number of] counties, districts and authorities in . . . states and entrepreneurial behavior on their part in the public sector has frequently played a major role in the establishment of the infrastructure necessary for economic development. They provide tax and debt capacities, some degree of functional professionalization, and officials whose record for reelection or career advancement depends upon the production of public goods and services.[62]

There is a growing literature that attempts to create a political economy of governmental jurisdictions.[63]

A normative theory of federalism should be concerned with the size and number of organizational units, and the areas within which they ought to operate so as to enhance the quality of public services. If it were in fact true that better education, or police or welfare services are provided in larger units, states would be superior to counties, which would overwhelm cities, and all would lose out entirely to the central government. In fact, there appear to be no economies of scale whatsoever for most services. In elementary and secondary education, and in regard to crime, smaller appears to be better. It may be that specialization among police, like police laboratories, gathers headlines but is inefficient, whereas placing almost all police on the streets as in small jurisdictions deters more crime or makes citizens feel safer. Smaller schools may lead to greater interpenetration of school and parental values. "In summary," according to Niskanen and Levy, "the evidence developed by all the major studies in the last twenty years—by numerous scholars using different techniques and different data sources—is consistent and, in total overwhelming: there do not appear to be any significant economies of scale in the provision of local government services (other than water and sewage services) above the level of the smaller cities."[64]

On the contrary, there are now bits of positive evidence that the quality of service declines (below a minimum level) with increasing size. Using a variety of measures of student performance in California, for example, Niskanen and Levy find that "School district size has a consistent *negative* relation to student performance."[65] And Elinor Ostrom has shown that smaller police departments either perform better or do no worse than larger ones on a variety of measures.[66]

Now the nature of the governmental sanction and the service to be performed is evidently important. Defense and foreign policy are not usually made on the state plane; there are constitutional provisions against it. But wait a minute. We are talking about the federal principle in regard to size and number and not the division of authority. Several armed services departments might not be better than a single one. Defense, indeed, precisely because it appears inappropriate, might well serve as a microcosm of the macro-errors we wish to expose. Unification of the armed forces after the end of the Second World War was proposed on the basis of securing extra efficiency by increasing economies of scale and by central control to avoid overlap and duplication. When a public organization like defense is several times larger than the largest private corporation, and spends tens of billions of dollars, the argument of efficiency must be based on self-delusion. Who can understand what actually goes on in so overwhelmingly large an organization? (Saying Department of Defense is not equivalent to encompassing it in an individual or an organizational mind and memory!)

Achieving efficiency (which is always problematical) ought not to have been the main issue—at least not to me. Achieving creativity in concepts of defense and civilian control over the armed forces should have been the main concerns. For these purposes, diversity was far better than uniformity, pluralism preferable to unity. Suppose there were, instead of the old three services, a new hexagonal armed forces—the old army, navy, air force and marines, together with a new agency for procurement and one for production of weapon systems. The question of control by civilian outsiders would have been more readily answered because the quarrel among the six services would have revealed the most interesting secrets. Creativity would, I think, have been better served because of the incentive for each service to compete with the other to show that it could do whatever was worth doing in a better way. The separation between procurement and production, moreover, would have reduced collusion between armed forces and industry because the designer and the producer would have been different; at the same time, competition would have increased both for creating the best design and for producing the best weapon according to that design. Coercing the services under the guise of a cooperative Department of Defense may satisfy appearances of neatness. The actuality of control and creativity that could have come from the consent supplied by conflict, however, though messy, would have better served our country.

Advocates of federalism should start with the supposition that smaller is superior. At least, they should consider that as a leading hypothesis. The hypothesis may, under some conditions, be invalid. But it should always be the leading hypothesis—a bias I called it earlier—of people who profess to prefer federalism.

Notes

1. William T. Goldman, "Organizing for State and Multi-State Development Planning," mimeograph, 1968, p. 55.
2. Ibid., p. 14.
3. Ibid., pp. 14–15.
4. Ibid., p. 50.
5. Ibid.
6. Carlisle P. Runge and W.L. Church, "New Directions in Regionalism: A Case Study of Intergovernmental Relations in Northwestern Wisconsin," *Wisconsin Law Review*, 1 (1971): 453–454.
7. Ibid., p. 495.
8. Ibid., p. 509.
9. Ibid., p. 511.
10. Ibid., pp. 515–516.
11. Ibid., p. 517.
12. James L. Sundquist (with the collaboration of David W. Davis), *Making Federalism Work: A Study of Program Coordination at the Community Level* (Washington, D.C.: The Brookings Institution, 1969), p. 242.
13. Ibid., p. 273.
14. Ibid., p. 274.

15. Ibid., p. 278.
16. Ibid., p. 272.
17. Ibid., p. 271.
18. Ibid., p. 268.
19. Ibid., pp. 243–244.
20. Ibid., p. 244.
21. Ibid., pp. 244–246.
22. Ibid., pp. 247–248.
23. Ibid., pp. 248–249.
24. Ibid., p. 249.
25. Ibid., p. 250.
26. Ibid.
27. Robert Warren, "Alternative Governmental Structures for Area Development," mimeograph, p. 6.
28. Robert Warren and Geoffrey Wandesford-Smith, "Federal-State Development Planning: The Federal Field Committee for Development Planning in Alaska," mimeograph, p. 16.
29. Ibid., p. 17.
30. Ibid., p. 28.
31. Ibid.
32. William Riker, *Federalism: Origin, Operation, Significance* (Boston: Little, Brown and Company, 1964).
33. Aaron Wildavsky (ed.), *American Federalism in Perspective* (Boston: Little, Brown and Company, 1967).
34. William Anderson, "Federalism and Intergovernmental Relations, A Budget of Suggestions for Research" (prepared for the Committee on Public Administration and the Committee on Government of the Social Science Research Council, Chicago, 1946); also, *The National and the States, Rivals or Partners?* (Minneapolis: University of Minnesota Press, 1957).
35. S. Rufus Davis, *The Federal Principle: A Journey through Time in Search of a Meaning* (Berkeley: University of California Press, 1978) is a superb survey of futile efforts from ancient to modern times.
36. Eugene Smolensky, Richard Burton, and Nicolaus Tideman, "An Operational Approach to an Efficient Federal System, Part I, On the Specification of Horizontal Relationships," mimeograph.
37. Ibid., p. 1.
38. Ibid., p. 2.
39. Ibid.
40. Ibid., p. 4.
41. Ibid., pp. 5, 8.
42. Ibid., p. 20.
43. Ibid., pp. 23–24.
44. Ibid., pp. 24–25.
45. Ibid., p. 3.
46. Stephen Cohen, "Planning in Essex County, New York: An Analysis of the Current EDA Approach to Planning in Rural Areas, and Some Suggestions for Reforms," mimeograph, p. 640.
47. Ibid., p. 643.
48. Ibid., pp. 645–646.
49. Ibid., p. 651.
50. Pierre Clavel, "The Politics of Planning: The Case of Non-Metropolitan Regions," mimeograph, p. 25.

51. Samuel M. Leadley, "Organizational Innovation: Case Study in Planning and Development," mimeograph.
52. Ibid., p. 15.
53. Ibid., p. 16.
54. Ibid.
55. Ibid., p. 17.
56. Ibid.
57. Ibid.
58. Ibid., p. 18.
59. Ibid.
60. Ibid.
61. Ibid., p. 23.
62. Robert Warren and Geoffrey Wandesford-Smith, "Federal State Development Planning."
63. These issues are splendidly posed in Elinor Ostrom's "Metropolitan Reform: Propositions Derived from Two Traditions," *Social Science Quarterly*, 53 (December 1972): 474–93. See also Vincent Ostrom and Elinor Ostrom, "Public Choice: A Different Approach to the Study of Public Administration," in *Public Administration Review*, 31, no. 2 (March/April 1971): 203–216. Vincent Ostrom, Charles M. Tiebout, and Robert Warren, "The Organization of Government in Metropolitan Areas: A Theoretical Inquiry," *American Political Science Review*, 55 (December 1961): 831–842; Robert Warren, *Government in Metropolitan Regions: A Reappraisal of Fractionated Political Organization* (Davis: Institute of Governmental Affairs, University of California, Davis, 1966); Robert Bish, *The Public Economic of Metropolitan Areas* (Chicago: Markham Press, 1971); Jerome Rothenberg, "Strategic Interaction and Resource Allocation in Metropolitan Intergovernmental Relations," *American Economic Review*, 59 (May 1969): 494–503; Bryan Ellickson, "Jurisdiction Fragmentation and Residential Choice," *American Economic Review*, 61 (May 1971): 334–339; Wallace E. Oates, "The Effects of Property Taxes and Local Spending on Property Values: An Empirical Study of Tax Capitalization and the Tiebout Hypothesis," *Journal of Political Economy*, 77 (December 1969): 957–971; and the literature cited in the papers by Elinor Ostrom and by Vincent Ostrom and Elinor Ostrom, op. cit.
64. William Niskanen and Mickey Levy, "Cities and Schools: A Case for Community Government in California," Graduate School of Public Policy Working Paper no. 14 (Berkeley: University of California, June 1974), p. 22.
65. Ibid., p. iv.
66. Elinor Ostrom and Gordon P. Whitaker, "Community Control and Governmental Responsiveness: The Case of Police in Black Communities," in *Improving the Quality of Urban Management* , eds. David Roger and Willis Hawley, vol. 8, *Urban Affairs Annual Review* (Beverly Hills: Sage Publications, 1974), pp. 303–304; Elinor Ostrom and Roger B. Parks, "Suburban Police Departments: Too Many or Too Small?" in *Urbanization of the Suburbs*, Louis H. Masotti and Jeffrey K. Hadden, eds., vol. 7, *Urban Affairs Annual Review* (Beverly Hills: Sage Publications, 1970), pp. 367–402; Elinor Ostrom, "Size and Performance in a Federal System," *Publius*, 4, no. 4 (1974); Elinor Ostrom, William H. Baugh, Richard Guarasci, Roger B. Parks, and Gordon P. Whitaker, *Community Organization and the Provision of Public Services*, Administrative and Policy Studies Series (Beverly Hills: Sage Publications, 1973).

3

Federalism Means Inequality

Federalism is in decline because it cannot be sustained without the underlying support of political culture. From its beginnings until this very day, there have been two classic criticisms of the structure of American federalism: it is too strong or too weak. Either the structure is a sham (federalism as a front for a unitary state) or the structure is stultifying (federalism as an obstacle to effective government).

These criticisms have been countered by two styles of argument: political geometry and political sociology. The geometricians take the structural thesis head on. They argue, for example, that federal structure is built into national policymaking so the central government is effectively prevented from subsuming state governments. Or they contend that the diversity of state governments aids implementation of policy by providing a proper variety of responses to local conditions. Or they say that federal structure tames conflict by diverting it into many small ones, occurring at different times and in various places. The argument from political sociology, by contrast, simply states that structure need not and does not equal function. Between structure and function, they say, lies society, which both bolsters federalism by representing social differences within geographic locations, and mitigates its excesses by connecting the constitutional parts. The institutional form of political sociology was political parties. The tendencies to formal dispersion of power would be met by informal concentration in parties.

I will consider two explanations for the loss of vigor (the structure remains but its social support weakens) in the federal system: the decline of political parties and the rise of a sectarian political culture dedicated to equality of results. All the perspectives, whether structural or social, supportive or critical, centralizing or decentralizing, share a set of assumptions that have increasingly come into question. As usual, the main assumption was that life would remain unchanged. Government would remain small. For most of American history the question of federal finance was what to do with surpluses, not deficits. Until some time in the 1960s, fiscal drag, raising too much revenue, was considered the big problem. Government that used up a third or more of citizen income or employed a fifth or more of the people or operated hundreds of programs and bureaus was unthinkable. So was the welfare state. So were modern technology, communications, and mass mobility.

Most unimaginable of all, these technical and demographic changes resulted in a fundamental change in the direction of political causality. Until recently, everyone's model was that citizens (alone or in groups) put pressure on government, which then responded well or badly. It was not government that pressured the people but the other way around. A great leader might manage to rouse people to a pitch of patriotism, but this was a sometime thing, saved for special occasions like the good family china, lest through overuse its essential fragility lead to breakage. No one, it is safe to say, contemplated government setting up institutions to put pressure on it.

Before our eyes, the time that waits for no one destroyed these traditional arguments pro and con about American federalism. So swiftly that we barely caught a glimpse of what was happening as it passed us by, the premises of the debate shifted. In a phrase, plane political geometry became solid. The theory of dual federalism, in which the parts never penetrated except by benefit of constitutional clergy, was in disarray. So long as the image of the layer cake prevailed, a platonic arrangement if there ever was one, constitutional lawyers knew they should ask not only what was to be done but who was to do it. Parallel play, a space for states, a space for national government, a space for them together, was the neat theory. When Morton Grodzins[1] observed in *The American System* that these parallel lines really met in real life, there was complexity but not consternation. Daniel Elazar demonstrated in *The American Partnership* that cooperative federalism was the norm virtually from the outset.[2] There remained the good feeling that American pragmatism had apparently triumphed over arid theory.

The question of what exactly to call it was, for a time, superseded by calling it good. So long as a few bands of dark were still visible against the white, there was sufficient resolution to say it was something. We could have our federal cake (color me marble!) and eat it too. As government grew and as research became more sophisticated, swirls of marble gave way to veins going every which way, so crisscrossed that no one could say what was up or down or who was (simultaneously?) on top or bottom. How could we enjoy federal structure if we did not know what it was? The seemingly arcane disputes about a formula for designating the degree of federalism hid a deeper dilemma, for the political sociology of federalism fared no better, indeed worse, than the political geometry. After all, there was still the structure—states existed; senators could only come from states; and representatives ran in districts within states or the District of Columbia. But where was the social glue?

The social study of federalism talked about state and regional interests but rarely about values and practices.[3] It was assumed that American political cultures were compatible with (and were the expression of) the variety and diversity necessary to maintain a federal system. A belief in uniformity, for instance, could be manifested by strong central rule, modified by delegating authority to geographic units. This delegation, though it belongs to a unitary conception of government, is often called decentralization. Noncentralization refers to independent centers of power in geographic areas who do (and are expected to) differentiate themselves. Though there may be some centralization in a federal system, and there might be decentralization (i.e., delegation), there must be noncentralization. A belief in equality, not only of opportunity but of outcome, would be hostile to noncentralization, for then there could be no substantial differences among states.

Uniformity is antithetical to federalism. The existence of states free to disagree with one another and with the central government inevitably leads to differentiation. Yet states must differ if they are to do more than obey central directives. Were there to be a change in values toward equality of condition, the political culture that undergirds federalism would fall apart. You can have a belief in equality of opportunity to be different, but you cannot have a belief in equality of results to be the same and still have a federal system.

The special subject of political sociologists has been political parties. Though national parties were weak by European standards, parties in America were the only nationwide social support for the institutional structure of federalism. The decline of parties has not so much left sociologists unemployed as bereft of a rationale for why the unadorned federal structure should work as well as some of them supposed.

Weak Parties

The confusion and concern over what to call federalism is a reflection of a deeper anxiety over what it is becoming. In ancient times the ability to name an object or a person was equivalent to controlling it or the person. The Bible contains numerous episodes of Jacob or Moses or Manoa trying to discover the name of God and being told, one way or another, that this was improper. Brilliant studies of the definitions and metaphors used to characterize federalism in the past as well as the present, however, suggest that the difficulty may be inseparable from the enterprise. One recent author finds 267 separable designations. If federalism is so far out of control that we do not know what to call it, so is our government, and so are we.

The most visible measure of the vitality of federalism is the party system. If parties (almost always modified by the word "decentralized") were in good shape, so was the federal system. As long as they existed together, the question of causality need never be asked or, at least, answered. Did strong parties emerge from a strong federal structure or did strong parties create and maintain a strong federal structure?

In the mid-1960s I collected a number of the best pieces on federalism in order to give students the advantage of a convergence of thought that had emerged in the literature. One basic agreement leaps from that literature: the significance of political parties. William Riker, in "Federalism: Origin, Operation, Significance," put the case squarely:

> The federal relationship is centralized according to the degree to which the parties organized to operate the central government control the parties organized to operate the constituent governments. This amounts to the assertion that the proximate cause of variations in the degree of centralization (or peripheralization) in the constitutional structure of a federalism is the variation in degree of party centralization.[4]

Like other writers on federalism, Riker inserts a kicker: "It is theoretically possible but practically difficult to measure the structure of the party system."[5] If we cannot measure the structure of the party system, then how do we calibrate it with the structure of the federal system?

Morton Grodzins begins with the same confident assertion: "The nature of American political parties accounts in largest part for the nature of the American governmental system. The specific point is that the parties are responsible for both the existence and form of the considerable measure of decentralization that exists in the United States."[6] Almost as soon as that sentence has expired, Grodzins begins to equivocate. Life is complicated. Demands for action by the national government may be attributed on occasion to failure by parties within states to offer appropriate policies: "Thus, even with respect to decentralization, the consequences of parties for government are not simple and do not always move in one direction."[7] Causality is complex. "In the first place," Grodzins continues, "it can easily be shown that the causal relationship between party and government is a reciprocal one." Just as parties may shore up state structure, so may local control over nominations or the electoral college system, which are part of the structure of government, "'cause' decentralized government."[8] Though parties aid in achieving a decentralized government, "governmental [here formal constitutional] factors are partially responsible for the manner in which parties are structured. So government 'causes' the form of party; party 'causes' the form of government."[9] With so many factors potentially contributing to decentralized government, such as local attachments, geographic scope, and the wealth of the nation, which makes redundancy affordable, party can be only one of a number of statements on the subject endlessly modified. No one does this with greater sophistication than David Truman in "Federalism and the Party System." He says:

> In a federal system, decentralization and lack of cohesion in the party system are based on the structural fact of federalism. . . . Three factors derived from the existence of the states as separate and largely self-sustaining power centers—channeling the claims of local socioeconomic interest groups, inviting their use as leverage against federal action by interests which are only tactically local, and providing for competing and frequently incompatible nuclei of decentralized intra-party conflict . . . go a long way toward indicating that there is something in federalism which induces decentralization and lack of coherence in a party system.[10]

We discover that "the interdependence of constitutional forms and types of political party is a fact, obvious enough in its simple statement but complex and baffling when the observer undertakes to explain these interrelations as they bear upon past changes in the political life of a people or to anticipate the form and direction of developments in the future." In contexts characterized by multiple and reciprocal causation, where "the cast has altered the mold," we learn that a "search for origins and for trends is thus bedeviled by the tendency to treat in linear, cause-and-effect terms a relationship which is circular and elusive."[11]

So concerned is he with complexity that Truman refuses to speak of the "party system," saying that would prejudge the question of whether there is one or not.[12] A dive into the watery depths of federalism leaves everyone gasping for air. Yet there are one or two things on which we can grab hold. Up through the 1950s, at least, parties still performed the distinctive function of nominating candidates. Even as presidential campaigns become more centralized, "the power over nominations remains decentralized."[13] In understanding federalism, however, answers only lead to further questions. "The American party system," Truman continues, "thus tends to be characterized by decentralization of power with respect to its most crucial function, by structural confederation, and by a lack of coherence in matters of major policy. What have the facts of federalism to do with this? To what extent is this an inescapable consequence of the federal system itself?"[14] To this question Truman has an answer, which soon enough turns into its own question:

> The basic political fact of federalism is that it creates separate, self-sustaining centers of power, privilege, and profit which may be sought and defended as desirable in themselves, as means of leverage upon elements in the political structure above and below, and as bases from which individuals may move to places of greater influence and prestige in and out of government. . . [15]
>
> But, it has been argued here, the degree to which these become the dominant characteristics of the distribution of power within the political parties is a function of a variety of other governmental and social factors which are independent of the federal structure or are merely supportive of its tendencies.[16]

Though federal structure alone encourages "an irreducible minimum of decentralization and disruption in the party system," Truman tells us other factors in society must also be taken into account.[17] While it is easy to show that federalism has some sort of an influence on the party system, Truman concludes, "the important question of how much effect it has remains unanswered and to a precise degree unanswerable."[18]

I have gone through this maze of quotations to show that in the study of federalism every author takes two steps backward for every step forward. They all agree that party is the most important institutional force sustaining federalism, but how strong it is or why it is strong or how to appraise the various factors contributing to or detracting from its strength, no one knows.

Party stands for social support, the political sociology undergirding federal structure. When we ask how parties contribute to federalism or how federal structure supports parties, we are actually asking: (1) is there social support for federalism, and/or (2) is there anything more to federalism than the bare bones of its structure? If the answer to the first question is no, so is the answer to the second. No wonder students of the subject have become worrywarts. What, then, will become of federalism if it has lost social support but retained its formal structure?

Putting the question this way, as if federalism were at the mercy of unknown and unfriendly forces, entirely apart from human volition, is like going to the Delphic Oracle for a clear answer. In an ultimate sense, there must be more forces at work in the world than anyone can comprehend. Assuming that we citizens had something to do with it, we can ask what the people have done to their parties and whether these actions, of which there are many, may not have something to do with their dissatisfaction.

What has happened to our political parties that they have ceased cementing the American political system? Better still, we might ask not what our parties have done to us, since we now allow them to do so little, but what we have done to them. In words of few syllables, we have deliberately and by design separated parties from society.[19] In every way we could think of, we have cut parties off from social support. First and foremost, direct democracy through primaries has taken the nominating function, everywhere regarded as the primary purpose of the parties, away from party leaders. Why work in a party year in and year out if one has little or no say in who will be nominated? Expression by independent political entrepreneurs, attracting a temporary array of supporters, replaces deliberation by party leaders. Discussion in party caucuses and conventions among people who know the candidates is replaced by staged media events or citizens voting in primaries who do not know one another, who do not know citizens in other states, and who certainly do not know the candidates. Caucuses are replaced by "cash-register" primaries, mechanically ringing up the results. A sense of place among people rooted in local party affairs and connected through them to national candidates gives way to a sense of frustration from not knowing enough about the candidates and, because of the proliferation of primaries, not being able to keep track of them.

The other side of the coin of downgrading financial "fat cats" is that there is no one who contributes enough to have a say. Instead of a constituency of contributors to add to other constituencies of accountability, there is another kind of specialist, the expert in campaign law and accounting, whose advice must be heeded for fear of not getting on the ballot or even going to jail. Or there are sophisticated political action committees (PACs) who organize to press narrow demands but who have little or no concern for the integrative, across-the-board concerns of parties. Something in society has been traded for nothing.

All of us have noticed that campaign buttons and stickers are disappearing along with neighborhood headquarters run by neighborhood people. For this the financial restrictions are partly responsible, for the only way to reach people is to use the limited funds for television, radio, and other public media.

It may well be true that Jimmy Carter the candidate, as he claimed in 1976, owed no obligations to anyone. By the same token, it was also true that no one owed anything to him. When he got into trouble there were few defenders. When he needed advice outside his own circle, there were few party leaders on whom he could rely, just as there were few on whom he was dependent. Like other presidents, to be sure, Carter could set up a White House office for governors and mayors. But, under the guise of protecting pure local government from corrupting contact with national party politics, their elections have almost entirely been switched to nonpresidential election years. So they all have less reason to guide and constrain each other.

There is no need to ask why parties have lost their social roots, since it is the purpose of public policy and national party rules to accomplish just that. Were there states determined to do otherwise, they would be prohibited from doing so, at least in the Democratic party, by the enforcement of national rules. The federal principle, insofar as it relies on national parties based on independent territorial units, no longer exists. Why not?

Four Cultures

What matters most to people is how they live with other people. The critical questions are how individuals should behave toward others and how they would like others to act toward them. No one answers these questions alone; they are embedded in culture—the different forms of social relations and the shared values that justify them. Political cultures answer questions about life with other people: How is order to be achieved and maintained? How are the goods of this world to be secured and divided up? How is envy to be controlled, inequality to be justified or condemned, power to be exercised and legitimated?

The answers of a culture of hierarchical collectivism are to impose order through a division of labor in which larger and smaller decisions are parceled out to different people and reconciled by commands from the center. Inequality is legitimated by arguing it is essential to safeguard the collective, each element being taught to sacrifice for the whole. Envy is controlled by teaching people their place, by reserving ostentation to collective bodies, such as the state or church, and by examples of sacrificial behavior as the elite lead and die in battle. Wealth is created by saving to sponsor collective investment, thereby guaranteeing the collective obligation to the future on which basis past sacrifices are justified. Authority goes with position from the top down, the exercise of power rationalized both as an antidote to disorder and on grounds of expertise, that is, "papa knows best."

The culture of competitive individualism imposes order by maintaining agreement on freedom of contract. Leaders are chosen like every other commodity by bidding and bargaining. There is no permanent leadership (will leaders not restrict equal opportunity to maintain themselves in power?), only different leaders for different purposes. Envy is mitigated by showing everyone they can have their chance too or by blaming failure on personal incapacity or bad luck. For individualists, risk is opportunity, providing the winners can personally reap the rewards. By the same token, inequality of result is justified on grounds of fair competition. Where hierarchies can take long-term risks for future growth by characteristic techniques of shedding blame (secrecy, complexity, deception), individualists depend on markets to reward the most promising solutions while discarding the worst. Reliance on markets is legitimated by the claim that pursuit of private interests ultimately leaves everyone better off.

Taken together, the alliance of hierarchic and market cultures constitutes the modern establishment. From hierarchy comes order, including the rules for competition, and from individualism economic growth. There are, to be sure, tensions between them. Hierarchies care more about the division of labor defining who can do what, while individualists care about results, any combination of resources or people being all right so long as it maintains freedom of contract for the future.

The critical culture, the opposition to the establishment, is egalitarian. Where competitive individualism believes in equality of opportunity, egalitarians believe in equality of result. Egalitarians reject bargains that confer more gain on some than on others. Whether they be religious or secular, egalitarians choose to live a life of purely voluntary association. From rejection of authority come their other fateful choices. They choose equality because that is the only way people will agree to live together without authority. They choose criticism because painting the society outside in lurid colors helps keep their people together against the splits that must threaten those who live without authority. The reasons are always at hand: collectivism stands for coercion; individualism breeds inequality. Leadership either should not exist (hence the endless discussions seeking consensus) or it should be perfect (hence the appearance of the charismatic leader of unusual personal qualities in whom the spirit of the Lord or of perfect justice shines). Envy may be mitigated by surface signs of equality—plain food, simple clothes, sharing wealth. Since perfect equality is rare, however, envy is handled by expulsions and schisms as would-be leaders are driven out for usurping authority or they split and set up shop on their own. Wealth creation is not their concern, partly because they find it difficult, without authority, to tax their members, and partly because they can take that for granted, criticizing individualism for failure to redistribute the wealth that already exists.

By now it should be apparent that concepts of fairness differ according to the way of life each is supposed to support. For individualists, fairness is equal opportunity in competition. It is not success but failure (in theories, elections, or business) that is crucial, because markets for ideas or goods are regulated by dropping out the worst. That is why political democracy is mostly about getting people and parties out of office and has very little to say about what they should do when they get there, other than to leave gracefully when they lose. Fairness in a hierarchy is about following the forms specifying the relationships among the parts and the whole. Being treated fairly means being allowed to fulfill the responsibilities of one's station and supporting superiors to do the same. Fairness follows function in observing the division of labor and the boundaries between each specialty. The soldier must obey the superior officer, but the general may not invade the subordinate's home. To egalitarians, fairness follows outcomes; equal outcomes are fair.

Just as the various political regimes all believe in equality but define it differently, so they all believe in "decentralization." For collectivists, decentralization means delegation; for egalitarians, decentralization means central redistribution of resources among localities; only for individualism does decentralization mean competition among independent entities without central control other than by mutual agreement.

"Stolen rhetoric," as Mary Douglas calls values that can be shared among cultures because they do not point to particular acts—goodness, harmony, equality—also applies to "decentralization." Everyone appears to agree because the various cultures mean different things by these terms. Noncentralization, the independence of local entities from outside control, cannot be stolen by collectivists, any more than their talk about specialization and the division of labor can be appropriated by egalitarians who, in turn, can hardly use rhetoric about the social survival of the fittest. This rhetoric cannot be shared because it prescribes and legitimates specific behavior in the present, behavior so contradictory to some political cultures that they would self-destruct.

In discussing America it is especially important to observe the crucial distinction between individualism and egalitarianism. Both share a desire to live with as few rules prescribing their behavior as possible. Where individualists choose to maintain equality of opportunity to achieve distinction, however, egalitarians choose to escape authority by diminishing differences through equality of result. Thus the challenge the two cultures offer to authority is fundamentally different. Because egalitarians form part of a collective, they reject all outside authority. Because individualists have no collective ideal, they will join with anyone, including hierarchical authority, provided their ability to bid and bargain is respected. Individualists prefer minimal authority; egalitarians, none at all.

Though the United States is a single nation, Americans do not constitute a single culture. The attempt to explain the vast diversity of behavior observed in everyday life on the grounds of uniformity in shared national values is a major mistake of social science. Once we stop thinking that there are American (or German or Japanese) values uniformly distributed across the population, and liberate ourselves to think that varied ways of life may compete for allegiance within a national identity, we will be in a better position to gain self-understanding. When we ask about the mix of cultures within countries, we can ask what a change in the proportion of people who adhere to individualism, collectivism, or egalitarianism can mean for the country concerned.

A brief analysis of the compatibility of the federal principle with the major cultures (the primary colors, so to speak) will prepare the way for mixing subtler political hues. At the outset we will eliminate authoritarian cultures, ruled by a single hierarchy, and state capitalism, where competition has been driven out by state control of markets, as incompatible with democracy.

Within a democratic government, rival hierarchies might compete for office but they do not so much share as delegate authority. An areal delegation of administrative authority, as in prefectures, is not the same as the independent centers of power, at least in regard to some important matters, required in a federal system. At its extreme, competitive individualism is no more compatible with a division of authority between the center and the states than is hierarchical collectivism, for competitive markets, except for maintenance of freedom of contract, do not recognize a center.[20] They are inherently noncentralized. Egalitarians could accept either central rule where all individuals were equal or a confederacy where all states were equal, but not both, because one level of government would have to have more power over certain objects and, therefore, subjects, than others. Their overriding desire to secure equality of results rules out any arrangement, like federalism, that prizes diversity. My hypothesis is that only hybrid regimes, combining at least two cultures (and, of necessity, their differing values and practices) can support federalism.

Hybrid Regimes

Markets and hierarchies are the prototypical combination of centralization and noncentralization. Markets bring not only economic growth but also a belief in competition for its own sake. Hierarchy contributes authority and the stability to help make markets work. Both regimes, it should be stressed, institutionalize inequality, the hierarchy building it in beforehand as the price of order, markets encouraging it afterward as the main incentive for economic activity. This very tolerance (even encouragement) of inequality facilitates the diversity that lies at the heart of federalism. It is no deviation from principle for states to differ from one another and from the central government. It is inequality of result, not merely in income (some states choosing high tax, high services, others the opposite) but also in lifestyle, that distinguishes federalism as a living system from federalism as a front for unitary power.

Egalitarians could compromise. They could combine with hierarchy, accepting the coercion inherent in authority in order to use the power of government to redistribute resources and otherwise enhance equality among citizens. Alternatively, egalitarians might move toward individualism, accepting inequality of reward in order to escape from the involuntary authority of hierarchy. Actually, we do observe egalitarians in conflict between social democracy (collectivism and egalitarianism) and "small is beautiful" (individualism and egalitarianism). In the United States hierarchy has been weak but egalitarianism has been strong.

The historic egalitarian stance (beginning long before the anti-federalist and continuing until the 1930s), that central government—the hierarchical principle—imposed artificial inequity on society, predisposed its adherents to an alliance with individualists in favor of state government and in opposition to the national executive power. Where individualism is the dominant regime, as in the United States, egalitarians can reduce cultural dissonance (that is, maintain coherence in shared values and practices) by arguing that pure and unfettered competition, if actually practiced, would diminish differences among people. Equality of opportunity would then fulfill its promise by achieving equality of result.

Where collectivism is the dominant political culture, as in most European countries, egalitarianism can overcome its internal dissonance by arguing that acceptance of authority will enable government to enforce sacrifices from the better off by redistribution of income to the worse off. Egalitarian opposition to inequality is transmuted into the positive use of authority to achieve not merely equality before the law, which is the norm of hierarchy, but substantive equality of result.

The egalitarian impulse is noncentralist. Based on purely voluntary organization, distrusting authority, suspicious of expertise, preferring face-to-face relations in small groups without social differentiations, egalitarians could support not delegation of authority, which only makes it more remote, but noncentralization—small communities independent of the center. But—and there's the rub!—local discretion means local differences and differences imply that everyone is not being treated the same. Thus they are conflicted between their desire for active participation, which implies an alliance with individualists, and their repugnance for inequality, which implies a cultural coalition with hierarchy.

So long as collectivism (of the right or left) remains the dominant political culture in Europe, the chances for noncentralization, for a genuine expansion of local autonomy, will remain slim. When conservative governments are in power, the social democratic opposition calls for transfer of functions to regions (noncentralization) where their power is greater. When social democrats are in office, they speak of decentralization, that is, delegation of powers in order to spread egalitarian policies around from the center. So long as hierarchy dominates individualism, decentralization will remain a euphemism for delegation, that is, if I may abuse the expression, centralization "with a human face." The status quo will remain—talk of decentralization and practice of recentralization.

What about the United States? If federalism has not been entirely synonymous with American society, a symbol of its diversity and decentralization, it has long been equivalent to American government. In popular parlance, whenever the glories or defects of the peculiar American form of government are discussed, the name is federalism. When American government appears to be doing well, the cause is found in its federal arrangements. If those arrangements include the separation of powers and checks and balances, are not these also modes of dividing and containing power? If there are two of everything— legislatures, executives, courts, levels of government—is it not wonderful that the competition this creates produces order out of chaos? When we like it, this Noah's ark of ours is a marvelous compendium of unity amid diversity. When things are going badly, and the parliamentary is preferred to the presidential model, a unitary to a federal form, the blame is placed on federalism. Then there are too many rather than too few governments, confusion instead of cohesion, redundancy instead of rationality, so federalism is found wanting. When, for instance, a president finds a malaise in the country, we know he is finding it hard to govern. He has too little, not too much power, too many, not too few competitors: federalism is failing. Why?

What is that we hear rattling around in the closet of American government? The bare bones of federal structure. The critics' conception of federalism as a structure without a sinew, bones without connective tissue, has come back to confront us. At long last, the oft-repeated fears that federalism would regress to its constitutional origins, dust to dust, structure to structure, working out the consequences of formal arrangements unmediated by social ties, are being realized. It is not just that the demography of the states is becoming somewhat more similar; it is, rather, that the values and practices that would legitimate and rationalize noncentralization have grown weaker.

A mixed regime is compatible with federalism. Should either individualism or egalitarianism or hierarchy grow all-powerful, there would be no room for federalism. Should these political cultures coexist, the centralization of hierarchies and the noncentralization of individualism, accompanied by criticism from egalitarians, have proved to be viable. As long as egalitarians are weak, they add to the variety of organizational forces. Egalitarian groups tend to be small (large size is difficult without a division of labor), numerous (because they split often), and mobile (moving to get away from established authority). Unable to control central government, they resist its authority so as to maintain their local diversity. But if egalitarianism becomes stronger, so that it can hope to impose its preferences for equality of result on the central government, it will urge policies of uniformity. Some uniformity is one thing; a lot of uniformity is another. There is no escape from a compelling truth: federalism and equality of result cannot coexist.

Notes

1. Morton Grodzins, "Centralization and Decentralization in the American Federal System," in M. Grodzins (ed.), *The American System* (Chicago: Rand McNally, 1966), pp. 307–331.
2. Daniel Elazar, *The American Partnership* (Chicago: University of Chicago Press, 1962).
3. The main (perhaps the only) exception is Daniel Elazar.
4. William H. Riker, "Federalism: Origin, Operation, Significance," in Aaron Wildavsky (ed.), *American Federalism in Perspective* (Boston: Little, Brown, 1979), p. 56.

5. Ibid., p. 59.
6. Morton Grodzins, *The American System*, p. 254.
7. Morton Grodzins, "American Political Parties and the American System," in *American Federalism in Perspective*, p. 137.
8. Ibid.
9. Ibid., p. 138.
10. David Truman, "Federalism and the Party System," in *American Federalism in Perspective*, p. 107.
11. Ibid., p. 81.
12. Ibid., p. 85.
13. Ibid., pp. 87–88.
14. Ibid., pp. 91–92.
15. Ibid., p. 92.
16. Ibid., p. 107.
17. Ibid., p. 105.
18. Ibid., p. 96.
19. For a development of this perspective, see Nelson Polsby and Aaron Wildavsky, *Presidential Elections*, 6th ed. (New York: Scribner's, 1983). This is the major theme of Nelson Polsby's *Consequences of Party Reform* (New York: Oxford University Press, 1983). See also Byron E. Shafer, "Anti-Party Politics," *Public Interest* (Spring 1981).
20. E.E. Evans-Pritchard's classic, *The Nuer: A Description of the Modes of Livelihood and Political Institutions of a Nilotic People* (New York: Oxford University Press, 1940), is devoted to explaining how it is possible to have government without formal central institutions. He originated the term "organized anarchy."

4

Fruitcake Federalism or
Birthday Cake Federalism

Parallel play, a space for states, a space for national government, a space for them together, was once the neat theory of the American federal system. Under the prevailing image of the layer cake, a platonic arrangement if there ever was one, the parts never penetrated except by benefit of constitutional clergy. When Morton Grodzins observed that this parallel plane was really a triangle, a marble instead of a layer cake, there was confusion but not consternation. There remained the good feeling that American pragmatism had apparently triumphed over arid theory. The question of what exactly to call this compound of national and state rule was, for a time, superseded by calling it good.

So long as a few bands of dark were still visible against the white, there was sufficient resolution to say it was something. We could have our federal cake (color me marble!) and eat it, too. But as government grew from the mid-1960s, bands of marble gave way to veins going every which way, so criss-crossed that no one could say what was up or down or who was (simultaneously?) on top or bottom. Big Government (large numbers of large programs taking a larger proportion of national income) had made the division of powers between governments unrecognizable; it was hard to tell one level apart from another or (say, with the federal government supporting local libraries) to discern any difference in principle between them.

In its final peroration, a summary of its summaries, on the "Federal

Role in the Federal System," the staff of the Advisory Commission on Intergovernmental Relations concludes on a plaintive note. Harking back to its desire to name (if not tame) the federal beast, the ACIR staff says that the intergovernmental system "has become too big, too broad, and too deep for effective operation or control. Where all responsibilities are shared, no one is truly responsible. And, if everyone is responsible for everything, no one can fulfill their obligations."[1]

What kind of federal cake is this? Apparently, the layer cake and the marble cake have been succeeded by the fruitcake. Dual federalism (the layer cake) and cooperative federalism (the marble cake) now give way to fruitcake federalism.

At budget time it is always Christmas. The season is festive with anticipation. There are plums to be had for the picking. The closer one approaches the cake, fumes rise and the atmosphere becomes slightly alcoholic. One is sober enough to pick out the goodies but too drunk to notice how much one is eating. What has happened to these fruits of government spending? "Nutty as a fruitcake!" is not an inappropriate answer.

Who wants to be a fruitcake? This may not be the federal system Americans want, but the ACIR staff report suggests it is what they get. How else would one summarize their summary?

> Regarding *national purpose*, the record indicates that federal grant-in-aid programs have never reflected any consistent or coherent interpretation of national needs . . .
>
> Regarding *fiscal equity*, the record indicates that federal aid programs have never consistently transferred income to the poorest jurisdictions or individuals . . .
>
> Regarding *economic inefficiency* and *administrative effectiveness*, the record indicates that the management of intergovernmental programs in Washington and below is generally poor . . .

Purposes are incoherent; equity, in whose name most of this is done, is absent; administration is inadequate; and hostility between levels rises with their expenditures. If this is not fruitcake federalism, what would be?

All that is missing is the symbolic sense of being bogged down, congealed, suffocated, sodden, and shapeless. That too is supplied in the staff summary:

> Regarding *political accountability*, the record indicates that the growth of federal responsibilities has been accompanied by rising levels of political alienation, the increasing fragmentation of the political process, and the growing overload of

major decisionmaking institutions. The "system" has become incomprehensible to the public and even to most policymakers.

If Americans do not want to get stuck in a fruitcake, they might try changing the cook, but, in my opinion, they would be better advised to change the ingredients of their federal system.

What kind of federal cake would that be? For mature men and women that would be "birthday cake federalism," for they would be allowed to choose how many candles and calories would fit their self-image. Birthday cakes are individualized. Each person chooses the one they want. If they overeat, they pay the penalty. They do not eat other people's cakes and others do not eat theirs. Birthdays come at different times and are celebrated in different ways. I always thought that was what federalism was supposed to be about—diversity, variety, and not a little competition.

An Inquest into Old Glory

Instead of a minimum of political articulation, there is a maximum of public policy. The spheres of sectors of policy, such as housing and transportation, contain specialists at local, state, and national levels of government, including legislative committees as well as interest groups, universities, and think-tanks. They all know each other. But who, the question is, knows them? They unify policy in their own sectors. But who, if anyone, unifies the sectors? Thus, the old and persistent critique of federal structure as discombobulated—parochial, narrow, self-interested, uncoordinated—comes to the fore. The claim is made that single-issue special interest groups are running (or is it ruining?) the country. A federal system that used to glory in its diversity is now criticized for lack of unity; openness to the outside becomes confusion; competition becomes consternation.

What has happened to make the old-time glory of the American political system—its openness, its variety, its very unity in diversity—appear to be its principal defect? Before jumping to conclusions it is well to remind ourself of what the argument over federalism used to be about. The old argument was that federalism did not work well because it created numerous veto points that frustrated majority will. By the time the impetus for change gathered sufficient steam to mobilize support in all the necessary places, it had exhausted its reformist ardor. And even if there were policy, it had been so compromised in passage and so exhausted in administration that the confused child of implementation hardly resembled the sturdy parents of conception. The opposing position was that the modern anti-federalists mistook opportunities for obstacles. Their veto points, pro-federalists argued, were actually, in Grodzins' term, "multiple cracks" enhancing access to the political process. Federalism facilitated majority building out of minority interests. Federalism, therefore, meant more, not less, legislation.

Who was right? Neither and both. There were more vetoes of proposals but there was actually more legislation. Compromises cumulated almost always in the direction of larger size. The more big programs, it turned out, the greater the incoherence among them. Both sides had been arguing about the quantities of good legislation; both were swamped with quantities, period.

The result is federal structure without federalism. The existence of federal structure enhances entrepreneurship in program development. Every officeholder and bureaucrat, wherever situated, is encouraged to catch up with and surpass every other. At the same time, revenue sharing to the states guarantees that the question of what states would do if they had to raise their own money does not come up. Thus federalism as a doctrine for assigning functions to areal entities, or as a process of diversification through competition, goes by the boards. Competition for the same subsidies in substantive spheres of policy— the "picket fence" federalism about which Deil Wright has written— increases uniformity. In this "mishmash" which I call "fruitcake federalism" (that is, being bogged down in governmental plums and puddings), federal structure serves to multiply the offices and opportunities for increasing the quantity but not the quality of public policy.

Slowly the suspicion dawns that the old divisions may not be the new ones. As the states, the cities, and the "feds" fight over policies and payments, the people observe that all three grow larger. Perhaps what they have in common as governments is more important than what separates them. Perhaps the proper division is citizens versus government or the public versus the private sector. The growth of governments rather than the growth of *which* government thus becomes a major public issue.

The first clue to the appearance of a fruitcake federalism is the difficulty everyone has in deciding whether states, localities, or the "feds" have gained or lost power vis-à-vis each other in the era of big government. All possible answers, it turns out, are true in regard to some policies at some times but not in regard to others at other times. Can the federal government do without the states or vice-versa? Not really. Will states and localities refuse federal funds? Hardly likely. Will the federal government be able to cut the states out? No. A lot of noise is created by disputes over under- or overregulation. In the end, however, even as the participants wrestle, it proves impossible to separate them. And where they began the first round as lightweights, in the final round they are heavyweights. Perhaps, then, their relationship is not really competitive but symbiotic. If they live off of one another, the pieces of the puzzle would fit together: instead of more for one being less for another, as a static cross-section of time might suggest, a historical developmental model would show that more for one at hour "x" leads to more for both at hour "y."

My first thesis is that the size of all governments is more important than what they do. My second thesis is that citizens may be better served if we ask how to improve their choices rather than worrying over which level of big government should monopolize a service. Students of federalism should look not only at the balance between levels of government but, more importantly today, at the relative proportion of the public and private sectors. If federalism is institutionalized competition among governments, increasing rather than limiting citizen choice among service providers is its contemporary key. By sponsoring service providers of all kinds, by separating political demand from public supply of services, competition among governments may be enhanced. When the fruitcake gives way to the birthday cake designed for individual expression, when citizen choice characterizes federalism, the taste will differ state by state, which is as it should be if we want government to adjust to individual taste rather than adjusting the people to their government.

Symbiosis Instead of Competition, or
Why States Increase Spending

Policies feed on each other; the more there are, the more there have to be in order to cope with new circumstances, effects on other policies, and unexpected consequences. New legislative amendments and new administrative regulations become a growth industry as each makes work for the others. The policy sectors to which I have been alluding include not only the bureaucracies (federal, state, county, and city) that necessarily enlarge with the proliferation of programs and the interest groups and collective "peak" associations that lobby for whole industries, but also the burgeoning congressional staffs on legislative committees, appropriations committees, and the new House and Senate budget committees as well as the Congressional Budget Office. Bureaucracies generate corrections to old programs and ideas for new ones; lobbyists add their own. Congressional staffs make modifications as well as feed in ideas from policy communities outside, thus assuring a steady stream of initiatives. What part do states and localities play in spending?

Federal-state financial relations are a mixed-motive game. Each player wants the other to pay, yet each needs the other to implement the program. From time to time one side or the other appears to be in a better or worse position. In the 1950s and early 1960s, for example, state and local revenue appeared low in regard to central revenue. Indeed, the surplus in the social security trust funds, the increase in economic growth that multiplied the tax take, the running down of defense in relation to GNP, all worked to the advantage of the national government. A new term—"fiscal drag"—came into prominence. It purported to explain that the tax receipts of the central government grew so fast that this excess revenue exerted a restraining influence on economic growth. In order to get more spending into the economy, revenue sharing with states was advocated. Moving, for contrast, to the mid-1970s, it appeared that states were coming into surpluses while the national government was in deficit. In between times, one side would steal a march on the other as when certain states learned how to exploit social services payments. The picture portrayed is one of a semi-cooperative and semi-antagonistic posture, varying, to the frustration of neat categorizers, with the policy area, time, technology, and other factors too numerous to mention.

Viewed historically over time, however, these federal-state-local financial relations appear mutually supportive. Once the perturbations of particular times are taken out, the fluctuations smoothed, it is upward and onward. All levels end up taxing and spending more. Why is the trend over time so different from a snapshot at one time?

Because each financial "victory" is embedded as a base for future spending, and each "defeat" becomes a rationale to catch up, cooperation over time results in higher spending by everyone. While the players push each other down, it appears, they also egg one another on.

The mechanisms are well known, they have merely not been directed at the question of spending totals.

If imitation is the sincerest form of flattery, symbiosis—living off of one another—is superior. Suppose a state finds that federal matching funds distort its finances. The state has gotten into things which, while they may be desirable in and of themselves, lead it to spend more than it otherwise would. By the time this becomes apparent, a clientele has organized around the program. Entitlements or at least expectations have been created. One always unpopular alternative is to raise taxes, but perhaps a "nuisance" tax will do. Perhaps not. Other unrelated activities may be financed by loans or loan guarantees, thus making room. Or representatives in Congress may seek a larger federal share. Perhaps revenue sharing will fill the gap. Soon that also is committed. Other programs and other devices come into play. Two things have happened: state spending is higher and so is federal spending.

At the national level the plight of the states receives attention. Formulas are adjusted, deficits increased, loans raised, and tax rebates given. By and by the national government is hurting. It seeks to pass costs back on to the states. That is not easy to do. The "fiscal dividend" from the end of a war is absorbed. Each disaster becomes a rationale to come to the aid of the other and to shift costs across levels. Two things have happened: the feds pay more and so do the states.

Sometimes states are in good repute—closer to the people, innovative laboratories, decentralized—and sometimes the national government—talented, consistent, and egalitarian. Sometimes both are in bad order. Suppose the national government is suspected of being too powerful and the effects of its programs leave something to be desired. A brilliant idea occurs: why not have the states take the heat of implementation while the "feds" do the policy design? The federal government does not look as if it is growing quite so fast and the state governments appear more robust. Problems are solved by dividing functions but also by adding expenditures.

Budgeting by addition is the norm in intergovernmental relations. As George Break puts it:

> Although federal grant-making may appear to have progressed from specific-purpose funding to broad-gauge functional aid to general sharing of revenue, the fact is that each successive form has been added to the existing types of intergovernmental assistance.[2]

Evidently it is possible for some laws and regulations to pass through the supposedly impenetrable maze of government. Which ones? A good clue is provided by the noteworthy number of so-called accidental policies that turn out to have much larger cost consequences than anticipated.[3] How come the opposite error—much lower costs—does not occur? The answer is that when underpayments are discovered, something is done about them. But when overspending occurs, it is accepted as a fact of life. Of course, miscalculation happens; it is what happens to miscalculation that matters. It is not error making, which is inevitable, but error recognition and correction that count. Treating overspending as an act of God or, the budgetary equivalent, "uncontrollable" expenditures, is done accidentally on purpose. Since no expenditure need be subtracted from another, accidents become purposes.

The result of federal grants is not a state's independence to spend as it sees fit but state dependence on federal largesse. What William E. Hudson said about El Paso, Texas could be repeated throughout the nation:

> Instead of promoting local autonomy, the New Federalism grants—Revenue-sharing (GRS), Community Development (CD), Comprehensive Employment and Training (CETA), and Counter-cyclical Revenue-sharing—have helped to reduce city government autonomy. Since the early 1970s, El Paso's dependence on federal funds as a source of revenue has increased dramatically, local officials have become politically dependent on continued high levels of federal funding, and federal "strings" in the form of federal mandates affect local government activities more than ever before; the New Federalism has thus reduced rather than increased the city's independence from Washington.[4]

Birthday Cake Federalism

State and local governments compete to get the federal government to pay for their programs, and compete with each other indirectly for grants. Competition in the system occurs between states and between local governments to provide the best service/tax mix. This competition is *horizontal*. But policy integration is *vertical*, reducing accountability at every level. For what would state governments compete with the federal government? Responsibility for programs? Only if the other would pay. We can understand state versus state competing for taxpaying citizens or businesses—that's the diversity of the federal system. But the only competition between states and the federal government would be over (a) who pays the piper, and (b) who calls the tune.

What would be the incentives or rules for intergovernmental (i.e., vertical) competition? The relationship between states and the federal government is one of tension between rights and responsibilities. How is a balance to be struck? A formula is not in the offing. Governors have long thought about taking less money in exchange for fewer federal restrictions. How long this sense of self-restriction will last no one knows, but probably not very. The incentive structure still favors the states seeking federal dollars and the federal government imposing costs on states. With large federal deficits, this relationship is not likely to change.

This vision of variety might not be so bad: the federal government learns to perform a narrower range of tasks better. States learn to live with widely varying styles of life. People vote with their feet for the kind of life they'd like to live. In our time, perhaps that kind of active personal choice among lifestyles may be as good as we can get from government.

Any knowledgeable person can make a good (though not, of course, conclusive) case for federal assumption of a favored activity. The costs of medical care could be limited, for example, by exclusive federal financing, ruling out private or state local activity. The reason is that a lump sum, by limiting inputs into the medical system, would more effectively ration resources.[5] The relative priority of different programs is bound to cause continuous disagreement.

What, then, should be done if one desires a federal system that stresses variety, diversity, and competition? As usual, negative knowledge comes earlier than positive—big government is antithetical to federalism because it preempts resources for the national government, and because it causes virtually every activity to mix the levels of government. Variety in programs suffers as the feds seek as much conformity as they can get.

The point I wish to pursue about positive knowledge is that we don't need what we should not have. A cognitive approach through a formula for demarcation suggests that there is some general theory, known by some particular people, to which government activity should be subject. No thanks, for that would mean there must be activities not now ensconced at the federal level that should be there. Let us turn instead to setting up conditions for social interaction that are most likely to produce outcomes that can be described retrospectively as diverse, varied, and competitive—that is, federal.

Suppose some states offer certain services and others do not; one or the other will be disadvantaged. Exactly. That is what should happen in order to achieve variety and diversity. Maybe what is really meant is that some states will end up with all the bads—the poorest people, the noxious industries—and none of the goods. Then I suggest the people fire their incompetent politicians and hire competent ones.

Imagine states that keep out undesirable people and industries. Other states may then pick up their jobs and their people. A policy of ecology without people, or of people without industry, or of industry without either, makes no sense. Let people sort themselves out. No telling what they'll do. Why, they might even enjoy themselves in ways as yet undiscovered. Happy birthday, federalism, you finally can have your cakes and eat them too.

Notes

1. "The Federal Role, Criteria, Assessment, and Analysis," p. 173.
2. George F. Break, "Intergovernmental Fiscal Relations," in Joseph A. Pechman (ed.), *Setting National Priorities: Agenda for the 1980s* (Washington, D.C.: Brookings Institution, 1980), p. 250.
3. See, for example, David R. Beam, "The Accidental Leviathan: Was the Growth of Government a Mistake?" *Intergovernmental Perspective*, vol. V (Fall 1979): 12–19.
4. William E. Hudson, "The New Federalism Paradox," *Policy Studies Journal*, vol. 8, no. 6 (Summer 1980): 901.
5. See Aaron Wildavsky, "Doing Better and Feeling Worse," *Daedalus* (Winter 1976): 105–123.

5

A Double Security:
Federalism as Competition

"A double security arises to the rights of the people. The different governments will control each other, at the same time that each will be controlled by itself."
—Federalist No. 51

When we want knowledge, we do not set up a hierarchy whose purpose is to figure out the best way to learn new things; on the contrary, we rely on a competitive process in which numerous people, connected by common interests, strive for excellence. When we want liberty, we do not establish an organization to make us free; instead, we rely on political parties to compete for popular favor. When we want economic growth, we do not set up a command and control system, because we know that would be counterproductive. Rather we rely on bidding and bargaining among independent and interdependent economic agents to make resources grow. Why, then, when we wish to arrive at a division of labor between the national and the state governments, do we seek a central, cerebral solution, as if there could be some set of principles to be accepted by (or imposed on) everyone that would tell us what should be done by whom? If we think so well of competition that we enthrone it in democracy, science, and economics, why should we not tackle the problem of federal structure in the same way? What would a federal system look like if it were organized by rules meant to produce a division of labor that would reflect the results of competition?

A Prelude to Competition

Parallel play (a space for states, a space for national government, and a space for both of them together) was once the neat theory of the American federal system. Under the prevailing image of the layer cake (a platonic arrangement if ever there was one), the parts never penetrated except by benefit of constitutional clergy. When Morton Grodzins observed that this parallel plane was really a triangle, a marble cake instead of a layer cake, there was confusion but not consternation.[1] As Daniel Elazar demonstrated, cooperative federalism was the norm virtually from the outset.[2] The good feeling remained that American pragmatism had apparently triumphed over foreign theorizing.

The question of what exactly to call this compound of national and state rule was, for a time, superseded by calling it "good." So long as a few bands of dark were still visible against the white, there was sufficient resolution to say it was something. We could have our federal cake (color me marble!) and eat it too. But as government grew from the mid-1960s, bands of marble gave way to veins going every which way, so crisscrossed that no one could say what was up or down or who was (simultaneously?) on top or bottom. Big government (large numbers of large programs taking a larger proportion of national income) had made the division of powers among governments unrecognizable; it was hard to tell one level from another (say, with the federal government supporting local libraries) or to discern any difference in principle among the levels.

Under a unitary regime, states and localities carry out national instructions; the problem is how to improve their obedience. In a federal regime, states and localities are disobedient. The operational meaning of federalism is found in the degree to which the constituent units disagree about what should be done, who should do it, and how it should be carried out. In a word, federalism is about competition and conflict. Federalism is also about cooperation, that is, the terms and conditions under which competition is limited. A federal regime, therefore, cannot be coordinated any more than it can be controlled or coerced. Federalism requires mutuality instead of hierarchy, multiple rather than single causation, and a sharing instead of a monopoly of power. What you see is what you get: the dinosaur solution operates so that programs multiply without simultaneously increasing the intelligence of those who design and administer them.

If federalism is institutionalized competition among governments, increasing rather than limiting a citizen's choice among service providers ought to be its contemporary key. Citizens will be better served by our asking how to improve their choices rather than by our worrying over which level of big government should monopolize a service. Students of federalism should look not only at the balance among levels of government but, more importantly today, at the relative proportions of the public and private sectors so that competition among governments may be enhanced. When a citizen's choice characterizes federalism, which is as it should be if we want government to adjust to individual taste rather than adjusting the people to their government, the programmatic products should differ state by state.

What, then, should be done if one desires a federal system that stresses variety, diversity, and competition? As usual, negative knowledge comes earlier than positive knowledge—big government is antithetical to federalism because it preempts resources for the national government, and because it causes virtually every activity to mix the levels of government. Variety in programs suffers as the feds seek as much conformity as they can get. The point I wish to pursue about positive knowledge is that we do not need what we should not have. A cognitive approach through a formula for demarcation suggests that there can be a general theory to which government activity should be subject. Only citizens, through repeated iterations, can work that theory out for themselves. Let us turn instead to setting up those conditions for social interaction that are most likely to produce outcomes that conform to citizens' preferences.

The Federal Government as the Fifty-First State

The first thing is to reduce the federal tax to a considerably lower proportion of national income. This reduction is beginning to happen. It is permissive, and it allows states room into which they can expand if their citizens are willing to pay. The thing is not to prejudge the issue; when you do not know what to do, why do anything? Let the states pick up what they wish; let the feds give up what they can. And may the best government win or even, dare I say so, lose weight.

Second, we should think of the federal government as the fifty-first state, that is, as a source of diversity rather than uniformity. Why, the usual question goes, must the feds step in where states fear to tread?

Because, the answer always is, a uniform response is required. Since it is diversity that we desire, however, it would be better to ask whether citizen consumers have sufficient variety from which to choose and, if not, to add rather than subtract alternatives from the menu of public choices.

Is "interaction" a synonym for "inactivity"? Not necessarily. The federal government can act as the fifty-first state by encouraging variety through competition whenever it judges that another alternative ought to be offered to the people directly (such as competitive medical plans) or to the states (better service delivery).

Suppose no government wants to buy some good or service that some people deem essential. Presumably the program has failed an essential political test in a democracy. Suppose some states offer certain services and others do not; one or the other will be disadvantaged. Exactly. That is what should happen to achieve variety and diversity. Maybe what is really meant is that some states will end up with all the bads—the poorest people, the most noxious industries—and none of the goods. Then I suggest the people fire their incompetent politicians and hire competent ones.

Imagine states that keep out undesirable people and industries. Other states may then pick up their jobs and their people. A policy of ecology without people, or of people without industry, or of industry without either, makes no sense. Let people sort themselves out. No telling what they will do. Why, they might even enjoy themselves in ways not yet discovered

Division by Cognition or by Interaction

Where is the philosopher's stone of federalism, the demarcation principle between central and state functions that would rationalize a division of labor within the American federal system? Nowhere. Every offer to specify what is local and what is national, I believe, will founder on these facts of life: every national activity has its local aspects and every local activity has a national perspective. Any two incompatible objectives may be reconciled by a third to which they contribute, and any two that are complementary may be made contradictory in reference to their contributions to a third. It follows that no criterion of choice can be consistent in regard to all the legitimate political perspectives that may be brought to bear on them.

Vincent Ostrom states the competitive federalism project even more grandly, "we would have the emergence of human societies that no longer depend upon a unity of power to achieve coherence in patterns in human societies. Such an idea is of radical proportions."[3] Under this vision of variety, the federal government learns to preform a narrower range of tasks better. States learn to live with widely varying styles of life. People vote by moving to a place where residents carry on the kind of life they would like to live. Perhaps that kind of active personal choice among governmental lifestyles may be as good as we can get.

Requirements of Competitive Federalism

Once we give up on the idea of creating a set of criteria that will tell us which governmental activities should be determined at the national level, which by the states, and which shared, we are still left with determining the structural principles that would facilitate a competitive federal system. Because we are talking about politics not economics, voters and parties not entrepreneurs, votes not shares, analogies to markets have to be made with care.

Mechanisms of Selection

Since competition may be viewed as a process of evolutionary adaptation, I shall begin with the mechanisms of selection. Citizens vote in at least three ways to manifest their preferences about "who should do what and how much" in our federal system. First, they vote with their feet by moving from one state's jurisdiction to another, must as East Germans expressed their preference by moving en masse to West Germany. Motivation to move for a single reason only, such as the combination of taxes and services, is unlikely; other factors, such as climate, housing, family, and job, may figure importantly. Nevertheless, government may be a consideration, a factor amplified by the propensity of Americans to move in large proportion and often. Presumably, two things will happen. Governments will try to make themselves more attractive to people, and people of diverse preferences should be able to find niches that come closer to suiting them.

The second way for selection to be effective is there must be an incentive to diversify. One such incentive is the necessity of attracting and retaining people. Another is the desire of rival political parties to obtain and retain control of government by competing for votes. Those people who are interested in competitive federalism should want to make it as easy as possible for new parties to organize so as to preserve and intensify competition. For instance, these people should support legislation to remove restrictions on party organization, including a party's ability to endorse whom it pleases, to restrict primaries to citizens registered with that party, and to spend however much it pleases in support of its candidates. Because parties depend on developing loyalty, they should have every opportunity to place their brand on candidates so as simultaneously to sharpen competition among parties and to simplify choice for voters. Were it deemed advisable to assist weaker and poorer parties to compete in elections, state-supported floors would be preferable to ceilings.

For the same sort of reasons, no effort should be spared in making it easier for citizens to register, which is often the greatest obstacle to voting. Aside from the advantage that higher rates of voting give to the legitimation of the overall political system,[4] we see that the larger the turnout and the higher the proportion of those who engage in this competition, then the harder the political parties have to work at being competitive and the more certain (according to the law of large numbers) is the process of selection.

Four Conditions of Free Competition

Individual choice is also limited by the available parties and candidates, hence my previous stress on allowing freer entry to third, fourth, or fifth parties. It is neither easy nor necessarily desirable to mitigate the limitation on choice that stems from party organization of government. The voter may not be able to choose a list of favored policies because the vote is really between rival teams who come prepared with a list of preferences. In other words, voting is not like eating at a Chinese restaurant where you can choose courses from both group A and group B, but more like a French *prix fixe* menu in which the choice is only among complete dinners. Without cohesive parties, the voter may be able to act more perfectly expressive at the cost of losing the ability to give policy an across-the-board push in a desired direction.

Principle of Size

Perhaps we can get a clue from the criteria that economists lay down for achieving perfect competition. Lists vary. George Stigler says that the following four are most common.[5] Taking them one at a time, we find first a size principle: "A main requirement of perfect competition is that the largest firm in a given industry is to make a trifling fraction of the industry's sales (or purchases)." The idea is to prevent a single firm from monopolizing a product or service so it could set prices without competition. In recent decades, however, thought and observation have revealed that it is much more difficult to establish an effective monopoly than had previously been thought, especially with the march of technology. The pressure and effects that facsimile machines exert on first-class mail, that fiber optics have on telephone and computer services, and that long-distance transmission and pipelines have on electric power are but a few contemporary reminders. Opinion is not yet unanimous but agreement is growing that only government can guarantee a monopoly. Thus, in principle, there is no obstacle to a competitive federalism even if one competitor is much larger than the others in certain fields.

But the federal government can run deficits, thereby supporting activities beyond the willingness of citizens to pay for them. This handicap (from the standpoint of a competitive federalism) may be overcome by customary or constitutional limits on revenue and/or pay-as-you-go procedures. In general, such procedures, which now exist in the U.S. Senate, provide that (above a budget resolution that sets a spending ceiling), any proposed additional expenditure covering any of the thirteen functions of the federal government must be accompanied either by cuts elsewhere or by new revenues. In this way, the doctrine of "opportunity costs" (defined as the value of an object being determined by what one has to give up to get it) is made manifest. Because federal budgeting would be shifted from all pleasure (indulging this or that group) to pleasure mixed with pain (some other worthy group will suffer), there is hope that the federal government will restrain its ambitions[6].

Principle of Independent Action

The second condition of free competition historically laid down by economists, according to Stigler, is that "firms are assumed to act independently" in competitive markets.[7] Insofar as governments are concerned, the proviso must be interpreted to allow coalitions but to disallow coercion. States can get together with each other or the feds, but no one can order the others so that the recipient must obey. Certainly this condition is true among states. It is partly but not entirely true of the relations between the federal and state governments. The feds can make it next to impossible for the states to refuse its lead, but this is the exception. The rule is compromise, even rejection of federal rule. Should there arise strong national sentiment for uniformity, say in regard to environmental matters or welfare programs, however, it is doubtful whether this pressure could be resisted. I will presently discuss the grounds for uniformity. It is sufficient to reiterate that central government compulsion is irreconcilable with competition.

Principle of Knowledge

The third condition of perfect competition is that actors have "complete knowledge of offers to buy and sell." Partial to the Austrian subjective school of microeconomics myself, I think this criterion is right but overstated. After all, a basic aspect of entrepreneurship is the discovery of heretofore missing information of a kind that might not even have been available without the action of an enterprising economic agent. Study of command economies teaches me, however, the importance of market prices. Without them—that is, without widespread information on opportunities for buying and selling—much of the economy is limited to much less efficient barter, as Adam Smith showed long ago.

Proponents of competitive federalism want to help make information available about the relative prices of governmental programs. Evaluations of programs should be multiple, varied, independent, and external. Multiplicity and variety are essential to mitigate bias. It is the residue of repeated evaluations, such as of farm subsidies or rent control, that are persuasive. Much more needs to be done, in my view, on such subjects as the cost of collecting taxes,[8] the (dis)incentive effects, and generally what we are getting for what we are giving up. There is no magic in evaluations, which can be as contentious as the ideologies behind them. The trick is to present the costs and benefits in as revealing a manner as possible. Just as purchasing power parities are more revealing of standards of living than income per capita, so competition would be favored by creative comparisons of services versus taxes. The best comparisons are not cerebral but experiential: the ability to live in a state, to move, to try again, and so forth.

While another criterion, the divisibility of commodities, is not quite applicable to states, it is possible to distinguish states from each other. The greater the range of states' differences and the more distinctive each state, the easier it will be for citizens to choose among them. For large differences to be maintained, however, one must also accept inequality.

Principle of Movable Resources

The last condition-cum-criterion of perfect competition used by economists is that "resources are movable among users." Movability is more important than it might seem. If industry is required to use coal scrubbers so high-sulfur coal can be used, thus reducing use of low-sulfur coal, competition is ruled out. If Alaskan oil cannot be shipped to Japan, where it has the highest value, it must be sent where it can spill on American shores. For purposes of a competitive federalism, impediments to the movement of people and commodities should be diminished. Restrictions on international trade are harmful in two ways: they weaken the selective mechanism and they set a bad example for the federal system.

A Few Favorable Considerations, Maybe

A review of conditions and considerations relevant to competitive federalism suggests that while not ideal, they are sufficient. There are obstacles but not fatal impediments. And I think current events are uniquely favorable. The collapse of communism (with its overcentralized, command economy) in Eastern Europe and in the former Soviet Union make federal features more relevant than ever.

It may appear that the European Common Market is moving in the opposite direction—toward centralization. And in certain respects that is true. But by no means all. On the contrary, a common currency is a prerequisite for enhanced competition. "A striking feature of contemporary Europe," Giandomenico Majone begins his prescient essay, "is the parallel movement toward greater political and economic integration, on the one hand, and toward regional decentralization on the other."[9] Far from being at odds, "cultural diversity is the very essence of the European identity." As the Common Market exerts its homogenizing force, I agree with Majone, preexisting regional diversity likely will assert itself.

What appears to be an inexorable movement toward a world economy paradoxically places a premium on flexibility. The ability to manufacture and deliver on short notice and to provide small batches of made-to-order goods is now advantageous. Thus, as Max Singer proposes for Japan[10] (some people's ideal of an integrated national political economy), the center should be small with most matters handled at regional and local levels. In sum, one world implies many regions, and an even larger number of localities. And what better mode of self-directed coordination than noncentralized, competitive federalism?

Consumer Federalism

The 1990s will witness a struggle between rival tendencies over the spirit of federalism as the American form of government. The choice will be between monopoly and competition. Will government be based on a bureaucratic division of labor within policy spheres criss-crossing levels of government, or will there be competition over service delivery among a greatly enlarged number of providers? Putting the question in the context of citizen activity, will there be participation via bureaucratic instigation or via citizen choice among alternative bureaucracies?

Bureaucratic Monopoly

The French philosopher Alain once said that there is more in common between two parliamentarians, regardless of ideology, than between them and any citizen. Similarly, we may say that bureaucrats at different levels of government may have more in common than they do with any outsider. They share expertise; they make work for one another. Indeed, they cannot exist without each other. They owe their jobs, even their future opportunities to the solidarity of their spheres.

Of course, they do not entirely agree or there would be no reason to differentiate themselves. Their task is to adjust the system internally so that national directives are made tolerable to those who must carry them out in the field. As the participants move from and between the executive branch, Congressional committee staffs, state and local governments, universities and consultancies, however, they are less likely to be concerned about where they live now and more about the good opinion of those in their sphere who will determine how well they will live next year.

As citizens are sucked into spheres of policy, participation becomes co-optation. Hearings are held to soak up citizen energies as well as to learn to mitigate their objections. Intervenor status is granted so that the government subsidizes people to put pressure on it. There may be occasions when intervenors want less done, as in certain environmental matters, but for the most part, the more expert they become the more they want done in their sphere. Since the bureaucracies devote all their effort to these policies, over time they should be able to deflect and to shape what they hear from "the voice of the people." Whatever their differences, citizen and bureaucrat will agree that their sphere should be enlarged and that it should deal with its own problems.

Let us pause for a moment to consider the pass to which we have come. The actors are bound together by a common interest in spheres of public policy. The nongovernmental actors are organized by responding to governmentally created opportunities. There is music (or is it moolah?) in the spheres. Their operatives move in and out of governmental positions. They want what any red-blooded American interest group wants: government subsidy without governmental control. They bargain out a common set of regulations with which both can live; the price of program change, as we know, is program growth. Individual citizens are also organized, their activities ordered by the demands of due process, sequenced by the requirements of intervenor status, overwhelmed by the facts that become the common language of those whose places they must someday take in order to amortize their enormous investment of time and energy.

Contrast these marriages of convenience among producers of governmental products, including routinized objection to them, with the citizen or state as the unit of action. Here the object is to save time and attention while making choices responsive to diverse desires. If everyone has to participate in everything (or almost), normal life becomes impossible. If everyone has to be expert on everything, citizens would be driven by the demands of government. So would localities. If the same sort of time, attention, and expertise were required to participate in economic life, consumption would become all-consuming and no one would have a chance to make a living. Just as prices enable consumers to do well enough, or to comparison shop, so might governmental services be arranged to simplify rather than complexify choice.[11]

The basic proposition of big government, running across state and national lines, fortified by conventional administrative wisdom, is monopolist: governments should control the allocation of services to citizens within their jurisdictions without competition. If they had their way entirely, governmental agencies would all have the equivalent of the post office's monopoly on first-class mail.

In private industry the theory is competitive but the practice often is not. Following William Niskanen, then director of economics at the Ford Motor Company, we may stipulate that if it could get its way, industry would prefer competition among its suppliers and monopolistic access to its consumers. That is why it is necessary to bring external force to bear to assure competition. The same sort of pressure must be exerted on government if it is to give up its monopolies.

Consumer Federalism

Since the citizen is at the center of its attention, consumer federalism arranges everything to make things easy and understandable for him and not for bureaucrats. No one likes competition (after all, you can lose) except the consumer whose life is made predictable by the uncertainties imposed on others.

For the citizen, then, overlap, duplication, and redundancy (in this context, synonyms for competition) are not wasteful but wonderful. They enhance reliability of supply; if one supplier won't, another will. They cut down information costs; products may be distinguished by prices; they may be exchanged; and, given diversity, their mixes may be compared at the margins. Redundancy results in suppliers working hard to guess what citizen consumers want rather than the reverse. Competition is the better mousetrap that has a variety of units competing to beat a path to the citizen's door.

Anyone who has to deal with governmental agencies or who wants to apply for grants knows that it is useful to have a multiplicity of points of access and largesse. It is then possible to play them off against one another or simply to go to the most receptive place. Thus, individuals can sort themselves out among agencies with different rules, objectives, and personal predilections. Similarly, grievances encountered in one place may be redressed in another. There is no *a priori* mode of action that fits everyone; instead of fitting citizens into a mold, that is, requiring that they be uniform, it is better to demand that agencies be diverse.

Who is to say what is the appropriate scale of activities? Outside of a limited area, including perhaps water and sewers, many unsubstantiated claims are made for economies of scale. The division of labor facilitated by large size may suit certain specializations but is unlikely to result in more cops on the beat or teachers in the classroom or case workers in welfare.

The major movement in education in the United States after the Second World War has been the consolidation of rural school districts. Every study ever done shows that the larger the size, the worse the scholastic or social performance, no matter what measure is used. One understands that consolidation may be useful to state and national associations of supervisors or may reduce the number subject to governmental oversight, but it is a bad buy for citizens subject to it.

If producers of goods and services have to compete with one another, however, they may decide to be as large or small as they like, running the risk of inconveniencing only themselves. They are the ones in touch with production technology; they, not the citizen consumer, have the knowledge to make informed choices. If they deem it desirable to sign additional contracts to extend their service areas, or trade areas at their geographic margins, or agree to emergency support or loan of equipment, they can gain whatever advantage there may be in size without losing responsibility to the users.[12]

A consumer approach will lead to better, if not bigger, state government. Consider, for example, the quandary of state governments in dealing with pensions or disability payments (it is easy enough for the two to merge) for their employees. Given the normal operation of the political process, it is all too tempting to hide the true costs of pension provisions by pushing them into the future when another generation will have to pay. The future, apparently, is now and the result is huge "unanticipated" costs. The direct way of dealing with this phenomenon is to set up special committees to monitor retirement provisions. Several states have done just this. But, after the first flush of enthusiasm wears off, a return to business as usual may be expected. Contracting out, by contrast, requires no constant surveillance. Whatever other faults the agreement has, other people—the service providers—are responsible for "fringe" benefits. All the financial costs are on top, out in the open. The relationships are easier to monitor, thus leading to more effective and responsive government.

Growth in Governments

If this hypothesis has merit, there should by now have appeared a growing size of all levels of government.[13] Size is sure. All levels—local, county, national—have grown rapidly in real terms in the last quarter century. Part of the puzzle of federalism is that while it appeared for a time that the national level was gaining at the expense of the state and local, the underlying trend is for all levels to grow, different ones spurting ahead then dropping behind but never declining absolutely or relative to national product. Perhaps, as Sherlock Holmes said about the dog that didn't bark, the clue is in what is missing, namely, no decline. As a general rule, the more different sources of funds—the more streams that flow into the river—the larger the output will be. By competing for control, by challenging the others, total spending is increased. By creating anomalies, inconsistencies, inequities, and inequalities, the levels (though this is not immediately apparent) work together to increase total output of spending.

The second trend, toward a larger number of competing units, requires evidence. In policy proposals, the signs of things to come are there. There are a variety of proposals, seriously entertained in Congress, for competition among medical plans, with savings shared among employers and employees. Voucher plans in education are live issues in several states. There has been a substantial growth in the amount of services provided by special districts, accounting for a decline in the relative position of localities in providing services. In libraries, mass transit, health, housing, urban renewal, hospitals, parks and recreation services the number of states with a multiplicity of providers has grown sharply.

An interesting change is taking place in the same 1,800 federally assisted planning units throughout the country. Their original planning functions, other than accumulating huge amounts of data, by all accounts have atrophied or never existed. These Councils of Governments (COGs, as they are sometimes called) or planning commissions or districts have taken on certain middleman functions between the feds and the localities. More interesting for us, however, is a noteworthy tendency for them to become entrepreneurs in their own right, offering for sale a variety of services.

Decongestion Requires Limitation

In a memorandum from Executive Director Wayne Anderson to members of the Advisory Commission on Intergovernmental Relations, dated February 20, 1980, he sums up the seriousness of the current situation:

> "Overload" of our intergovernmental system, which is predominantly the consequence of our bigger, broader, and deeper federal aid system, is the central and most pervasive intergovernmental problem facing the nation, our research richly documents. Decongestion of the system, we believe, is the foremost need for the 1980s if we are to improve the effectiveness, efficiency, equity, and accountability of all three levels of government.

How are we to achieve decongestion if the government keeps growing? Ultimately, growth at the federal level must be reflected in corresponding catch-up spending at the state and local levels. Were that not so (and it is hard to see how it could be otherwise with federal structure built into the legislative process), then the specter of the states being subservient to the central government might become a reality. But this, as social workers say, is not the presenting problem. The time when advocates of a vigorous federalism could take comfort from the sheer growth of state spending is past. True, there has been a much-to-be-commended invigoration of state analytic and executive capacities. They are, in general, more capable than their predecessors. Unless there is action to limit governmental growth, however, the very capability of this new generation, which naturally has an interest in its own survival, will convert a virtue into a defect.

Anderson's next comment deserves to be taken seriously: "In the staff's view, this federal role subject makes a very different kind of demand on the Commission than usually is the case because it necessarily involves discussion of our whole political system." The two problems—perpetuation and reinvigoration of the federal system on the one hand, and making government at all levels less monopolistic and more competitive on the other—are directly connected. As the song says, you can't have one (independent state and local initiatives) without the other (competition at all levels of government).

Unless the expectation of continuing governmental growth is stopped, one thing is inevitable: the intergovernmentalization of everything.

The virtue of the central government is uniformity: its laws should treat citizens the same no matter where they live. The virtue of state governments is diversity: their laws would be redundant if they repeated themselves regardless of locale. Stamping out carbon copies is something the center should do but states should not. What can we say about the conditions for these two virtues?

The first thing is that each maintaining its own virtue is a condition for attaining the virtue of the other. If states maintain diversity, this gives the center a stronger rationale—its lack is being made up elsewhere—for sticking to uniformity. And as long as some things are done on a uniform basis, there is a stronger rationale for varying others.

Reprise

If there are to be priorities, including a division of functions among levels of government, there must be a reason to do so and a mechanism for doing it. Yet there is no universally recognized theory or formula for a division of functions that could command assent. Under these circumstances—disagreement on spending totals as well as how to divide the money by level of government—attempting a cognitive approach under which correct decisions flow from agreed premises is not on. Instead, I have been recommending an interactive approach designed not only to implement but to discover what works best. The greater the number and variety of organizations for providing goods and services from government, which constitutes a competitive, citizen-centered approach, the better able the system will be to go one way in regard to this and another to that. The people do not have to postulate either the optimal size of producing units or the optimal pattern of spatial structure. Rather, these would be seen as the outcome of citizens, states, and localities getting the best deal they can, correcting errors as they go along, provided there is an effective financial constraint.

Would an approach focused on expanding choice of services be antifederal? Since this consumer-oriented approach does not rest directly on strengthening state governments, the question is bound to arise. To appreciate its relevance one only has to ask whether federalism is about structure alone and whether structure itself is about maintaining strong state governments. As posed, the question comes close to the position that federalism is allied to large government, the only consideration being that states grow apace with the national government. Thus, we are led again to consider what we conceive to be the essence of federalism, American style.

There can, of course, be no definite answer to a question that asks what we would like American government to be. My answer, it now should be evident, is that the genius of American federalism is competition, not monopoly. American history, origins, and development, I think, is misconstrued if it is conceived to be about monolithic structures—national and state—clashing by day, cooperating by night. Its key terms are separation and division. There never was a question about whether there would be states, only whether there would be a national government. The price of this national cohesion was containment through separation of powers within government and division of authority between different levels of government. Again, the key term is competition within and among the levels of government. Thus, if one is so disposed (and I am), a competitive approach may be viewed as an effort to recover the operative principles of American federalism under altered circumstances.

The twenty-first century will usher in an intensified cultural-cum-ideological struggle over federalism. Will states become administrative units of a nationalized polity to enforce equality, or will they become competitors for services and allegiances in a competitive political economy? Will the peoples of the world, having observed that central command is a self-destructive way in which to run an economy, decide to apply the same winning formula to the polity? The "double security" referred to in this chapter's title refers not only to federal and state relations but to the self-regulatory principles out of which the competing elements are constituted and renewed. Without an underlying belief in competition, including unequal results, formal federal arrangements will become a mask for national uniformity.

Notes

1. Morton Grodzins, *The American System* (Chicago: Rand McNally, 1966).
2. Daniel Elazar, *The American Partnership: Intergovernmental Co-operation in the Nineteenth Century United States* (Chicago: University of Chicago Press, 1962).
3. Vincent Ostrom, "Polycentricity: The Structural Basis for the Emergence of Self-Governing Systems of Order," in *American Federalism: The Constitution of Order for a Self-Governing Society* (San Francisco: ICS Press, 1990).
4. The United States ranks high in the proportion of *registered* citizens who vote but low on the proportions of *total* citizens who exercise the franchise. Raymond E. Wolflinger and Steven J. Rosenstone, *Who Votes?* (New Haven: Yale University Press, 1980).
5. George S. Stigler, "Competition," *The International Encyclopedia of the Social Sciences*, Vol. 3 (New York: Macmillan, 1968), p. 181.
6. See Wildavsky, *The New Politics of the Budgetary Process* (Boston: Little, Brown, 1988) for vivid illustrations.
7. Ibid.
8. James L. Payne, *Costly Returns: The Burdens of the U.S. Tax System* (San Francisco: ICS Press, 1993).
9. Giandomenico Majone, "Preservation of Cultural Diversity in a Federal System," in Mark Tushnet (ed.), *Comparative Constitutional Federalism* (New York: Greenwood Press, 1990).
10. Max Singer, "A Twentieth-Century Form of Government for Japan," unpublished paper prepared for the Japan-U.S. Friendship Commission, 1989.
11. See my "Citizens as Analysts," chapter 11, *Speaking Truth to Power* (Boston: Little, Brown, 1979), pp. 252–283; and "Citizenship in Science," in *But Is It True? A Citizen's Guide to Environmental Health and Safety Issues* (Cambridge: Harvard University Press, 1995), pp. 395–409.
12. See Robert Bish and Vincent Ostrom, *Understanding Urban Government* (Washington, D.C.: American Enterprise Institute, 1973).
13. An excellent introduction may be found in M.A. Sproule-Jones, *Public Choice and Federalism in Australia and Canada*, Research Monograph No. 11, Centre for Research on Federal Financial Relations (Australian National University Press, 1975).

6

What if the United States were Still Governed Under the Articles of Confederation? Noncentralized versus Federal Systems

A staple thought among historians of the years immediately preceding the American Revolution was how little revolutionary sentiment there was in the decades before. Through the 1740s, 1750s, and early 1760s colonists continually professed loyalty to the crown, if not to Parliament itself. Thoughts about the existence and/or desirability of an American nation did exist, but they were scattered. Early efforts to establish such a union were rejected on all sides, as we shall see, not only by the British executive but by all the American colonies. No doubt a slew of modern public opinion polls would have provided food for thought about national consciousness. In their absence, it is useful to discuss ideas that were written into colonial and later state constitutions.

Colonial Consciousness

A background feature stressed by Jack Rakove is worth keeping in mind: travel was exceedingly slow and most people did not move much further than their native province. When the revolutionary leader Samuel Adams left the city of Boston in order to take part in the First Continental Congress, for instance, it was the first time he had left his native province in his almost fifty-two years of life.[1] It took time for currents of thought to develop.

It is also well to note, as Onuf reminds us, that the republican-oppositionist ideology that fueled the Revolution was about getting rid of British power, not about establishing what in America might take its place or even whether there ought to be such a unified national power to take the place of the British king.[2] Indeed, I would add, opposition to executive power far away might readily be transferred to disapproval of national executives at home.

Let us, for the moment, place ourselves in the position of American revolutionaries engaged in a tactical struggle with the British. The revolutionaries' main point was that they had been denied the rights of Englishmen. How impolitic for them, then, to proclaim their own national union, a claim that would at once have convicted them of a gross contradiction and created needless controversy on a matter about which their supporters would have been divided.

Indeed, as Jack Greene has it, and many authorities agree, "Right down to the actual break with Britain, colonial national consciousness had been intensely British. All over the colonies, Americans took pride in their incorporation into the larger Anglophone world."[3] Benjamin Franklin commented as late as 1760 that the people of the colonies "all love[d] Britain much more than they love[d] one another."[4] If they looked to go anyplace, they looked to London and not to New York or Boston. Until the late 1600s, Virginia was the only royal colony on the mainland of what became the United States. The colonists placed greater store in charters they wrote themselves. These included the West Jersey Concessions and Agreements of 1667, the Pennsylvania and New York Charters of Liberties of 1683, the Fundamental Orders of Connecticut of 1639, and various law codes in New England.[5] These charters permitted colonists to create and administer their own local governments subject only to the proviso that they not be contrary to laws passed by the English Parliament, which was in any event preoccupied with other matters and much too far away: a return trip by sailing ship took a minimum of two months.[6] Governments under the charters were really groupings of counties and towns, each with its own local authority, which came together to satisfy the requirement that there be a single charter.[7] It is not so much that there were no domestic entity that stood over all the colonies, but rather more that state governments were largely created by localities rather than the other way around. This was not decentralization in which a national entity devolves its authority upon local units, but rather more noncentralization in which local units create larger ones.

Occasional plans to unite the colonies met with no support. The New England Council of 1643 was designed to deal with common problems of security. The various local governments acted independently of each other and the council soon fell into disuse.[8] The Commission of the Council for Foreign Plantations, devised in Britain, aimed at a mercantilist conception of milking the colonies for revenue. Paying no attention to existing forms of government in the colonies, this scheme for treating colonies as plantations did not get far.[9]

In accord with republican principles, colonists tried to keep royal governors on a short string. The Massachusetts story was typical. Starting way back in 1702, by which time the legislature (the General Court) had been in session for a couple of decades, the royal governor, as he had been instructed to do, demanded a fixed salary. To this the General Court replied that its custom was not to grant salaries for more than a year at a time. Amid threats and counter-threats over the next fifteen years, the British government threatening to revoke the charter and the colonists threatening to drive out the governor, a compromise was reached in which the colonists said they would vote the salary as the first item of business each year.[10]

A former Speaker of the New Jersey Assembly, Daniel Coxe, recommended in 1722 that a supreme governor be placed over the chief executives of the colonies, the governor having the right to veto policies made by a council consisting of two delegates each from colonial assemblies. The purpose of this body was to assign quotas of men and money for what was said to be the common defense. It got nowhere.[11]

The Albany Congress

The first semi-serious effort to provide a plan of union—the Albany Congress of 1754—speaks eloquently of existing conditions. The Six Nations of the Iroquois Confederacy were the most important of the nations allied to the British who depended on them to resist what they considered French encroachments. Existing practice had led to a series of temporary arrangements with existing colonies that satisfied neither the Indians nor the British. Always the British wanted the colonists to do more for their own defense, including better treatment of Indians. Always the colonial legislatures refused.

Meetings with a view toward some sort of union had gone on for over a decade.[12] At one of these meetings, as coincidence would have it, on July 4, 1774, the Sachem of the Indian tribes, Canassatego, aside from the usual complaints about unfair treatment and inconsistent policy on the part of the British and the colonists, all of which were true, recommended confederation:

> Our wise forefathers established union in amity between the Five Nations. This has made us formidable. This has given us great weight and authority with our neighboring Nations. We are a powerful confederacy and by your observing the same methods our wise forefathers have taken you will acquire much strength and power; therefore, whatever befalls you, do not fall out with one another.[13]

This recommendation led to a lengthy controversy in which the Iroquois Confederation has been variously seen as the model of the federal system established by the Constitutional Convention and a mere historical happenstance to which colonists paid no attention. The Albany Convention reveals no reliance upon the Iroquois Confederacy. Neither does the Constitutional Convention. The Articles of Confederation, though direct evidence is lacking, has a similar model in which unanimity is required for amendments. Indeed, the history of the Iroquois Confederation would be of interest mainly to students of noncentralized systems.[14]

The one certainty, which is that Benjamin Franklin made use of the idea of confederation and that he knew of the Iroquois Confederation, is also ambiguous in that his plan, as we will see, did not call for unanimity. In any event, the meeting in 1774 resulted in a treaty of friendship with the Six Nations between Virginia, Maryland, and Pennsylvania. Massachusetts and New York renewed an older alliance with these same Indians in 1748. Though all the colonies or provinces, as they were variously called at the time, were invited to a meeting in Albany in 1751, only South Carolina, Massachusetts, Connecticut, and New York sent delegates. They did not succeed either in persuading Indians of their friendliness or of doing more against the French.[15]

As war with France loomed larger, the British Board of Trade called for a conference of American colonies in order to prepare better for common defense. Commissioners from Connecticut, Maryland, Massachusetts, New Hampshire, New York, and Pennsylvania met with chiefs of the Six Nations, who were, of course, concerned about encroachments on their lands by all concerned. Based on a plan previously suggested by Benjamin Franklin as "hints," the conference agreed on a voluntary association of the colonies with "one general government," though each colony retained its separate existence. Administration was to be entrusted to the president general appointed by the British crown and a Grand Council made up of delegates from colonial assemblies.[16] Two noteworthy provisions stipulated that there would be from two to seven delegates from each colony depending on how much they contributed to the common treasury, and that legislative decisions had to be approved both by the president general and the crown. The jurisdiction of the Grand Council was confined to Indian affairs and to purchases of new land outside of existing colonial boundaries.[17]

As things turned out, the plan was rejected on all sides. And for the same reason: invasion of prerogatives they considered their own. The British government thought the Grand Council too great a power that might interfere with its rule. All of the eleven colonies of the time, some vehemently, rejected the proposal because it had direct taxing power over individuals. Though the colonies would have retained the right to decide whether they would furnish troops, the Grand Council would have been able to decide which taxes were the most convenient and how much defense expenditure was required.[18] As Franklin himself put it, "The crown disapprov'd it as having plac'd too much Weight in the democratic Part of the Constitution; and every Assembly as having allow'd too much Prerogativ."[19] Despite the revolutionary situation, Rakove writes, "Yet there is little evidence to suggest that any leader of resistance gave these matters ["the apportionment of power between some central agency and its constituencies"] serious thought before 1774."[20] Gordon Wood says the same: "Yet for all this exercise of continental authority, for all of the colonists' sense of being 'Americans,' for all of their talking of choosing between 'a sovereign state, or a number of confederated sovereign states,' few in 1776 conceived of the thirteen states' becoming a single republic, one community with one pervasive public interest."[21]

The Declaration of Independence

Study of the Declaration of Independence suggests that these summary statements are correct. One looks in vain through the Declaration for an unambiguous statement either that the states alone retain sovereignty or that there was an American nation to which sovereignty would be and should be given. One way out was the common assumption that the former colonies or provinces had always been "states" and remained unchanged throughout the revolutionary period.[22] True enough, the Continental Congress, established in 1774, exercised many of the attributes of sovereignty—establishing a military code of law, negotiating with foreign nations, creating and maintaining an army—that played into nationalistic sentiments. But none of that will tell us whether the states were prior to the union or came after. What we can know is what Yehoshua Areli tells us: "The concept of nationhood, then, was based not on the idea of intrinsic unity. . . . The establishment of a national government thus rested on the purely . . . utilitarian grounds of the necessity for dealing effectively with other powers."[23] As he puts it even more pungently, "In Europe the awareness of national unity created a desire for independence; in America independence antedated the will for national unity." Thus, "though the Declaration of Independence was issued on behalf of the 'United States of America,' the Thirteen Colonies considered themselves free and independent states which took over, separately and together, the attributes of sovereignty."[24]

Its title—"The Unanimous Declaration of the Thirteen United States of America"—nicely leaves open the matter of state versus national sovereignty. Such sentences as "Nor have We been wanting in attentions to our Brittish brethren, We have warned them . . . of attempts by their legislature to extend an unwarrantable jurisdiction over us," aside from the light they cast on what the colonists meant by attentions, leave open the question of who is meant by "We." The peroration refers to "We, Therefore, the Representatives of the united States of America, in general congress assembled" and "that these United Colonies are, and of Right ought to be, Free and Independent States" and "that as Free and Independent States, they have full Power to levy War, conclude Peace, contract Alliances, establish Commerce, and to do all other Acts and Things which Independent States may of right do." The emphasis is surely on the colonies as free and independent states, albeit in congress assembled. The form of government envisaged, if there were one, might be thirteen independent colonies or might be a confederation like the Continental Congress, but could not be either a unitary government or a federal government with an independent national government able to exert direct coercive authority over individuals.

Should there remain residual doubt of what was intended by the

Declaration, we have John Adams writing his wife Abigail: "Confederation among ourselves, or Alliances with Foreign Nations are not necessary, to a perfect Separation from Britain. That is effected by extinguishing all Authority, under the Crown, Parliament and Nation as the Resolution for instituting Governments, has done, to all Intents and Purposes."[25] States there were, foreign rule there was not to be, but a nation not yet. Historians are fond of quoting Patrick Henry's declaration to the First Continental Congress that, "The distinctions between Virginians, Pennsylvanians, New Yorkers, and New Englanders are no more. I am not a Virginian, but an American." There were many such sentiments. "But," as Jack Greene put it, "few Americans managed to shed their provincial identities and acquire a new national one so quickly."[26]

"Born Again" States

Stung by barbs to the effect that "you have no government, no finances, no troops," in 1775, in May of that year Massachusetts asked the Continental Congress for explicit advice about setting up a provincial government. Eventually the word came down: resume the Charter of 1691. Soon enough Congress told New Hampshire, Virginia, and South Carolina that they should form whatever government they thought necessary. Finally, on May 10, 1775, Congress authorized "the respective assemblies and conventions of the united colonies where no government adequate to the exigencies of their affairs have hitherto been established" to create new governments.[27]

It is useful to record here Lutz's summary of the first 18 state constitutions thus formed:

1. Except for Pennsylvania (1776) and Georgia (1777), the states used a bicameral legislature (Georgia adopted bicameralism in 1789 and Pennsylvania in 1790).
2. In all seventeen constitutions the lower house was elected directly by the people.
3. Although the percentage of white, adult males enfranchised varied from state to state, on average the percentage was eight to ten times what it was in England.
4. Of the sixteen constitutions using bicameralism, all but one had the Senate elected directly by the people, usually by the same electorate for both houses. Maryland voters elected an electoral college, which in turn elected the Senate.
5. With only one exception (South Carolina, 1776), all constitutions provided that the lower house be elected annually.

6. Of the sixteen bicameral constitutions, ten had annual elections for the Senate, and three had staggered, multi-year terms.
7. Nine of the constitutions had the executive elected by the legislature, and six more used a popular election essentially to identify the major candidates from among whom the legislature picked the governor.
8. Fourteen constitutions provided for annual elections of the governor, two for biennial elections, and two for triennial elections.
9. Twelve of the constitutions required voters to own property, usually between twenty and fifty acres or the equivalent, four required them to be taxpayers, and two had no property requirement.
10. Of the sixteen bicameral legislatures, thirteen had the same property requirements to vote for the upper house as for the lower house.
11. Of the nine states that involved the people in selecting the governor, eight required the same amount of property to vote for the executive as to vote for the lower house.
12. All but two of the constitutions required ownership of property to run for the legislature, with few exceptions requiring more property to run for office than to vote.
13. Ten of the sixteen bicameral legislatures required more property to run for the upper house than for the lower house, and usually even more property was required to run for governor.
14. Except for Massachusetts, Connecticut, and Rhode Island, which initially operated as states under colonial charters, and two states that wrote constitutions before the Declaration of Independence (New Hampshire, 1776; South Carolina, 1776), most early state constitutions included bills of rights.
15. With only two consistent exceptions, the rights listed in the bills of rights, including the right to property, were alienable by the legislature (the exceptions were the right to free exercise of religion and the right to trial by jury).
16. Thirteen of the seventeen constitutions were written by the respective state legislatures, usually after an election in which it was made clear that the new legislature would also write a new constitution. Only two constitutions, Massachusetts in 1780 and New Hampshire in 1784, were written by a convention elected solely for that purpose and submitted to the people for ratification.
17. Only four constitutions in the first wave mention an amendment process, and in two of those instances the legislature is the amending agent. During the second wave, an amendment process is mentioned more frequently, but except for Massachusetts and New Hampshire—which give the amendment power to the people—the power is invariably given to the legislature.[28]

The legislative supremacy gained in earlier decades was maintained in the new constitution.[29] By and large, executives were elected by legislatures through a joint ballot of two houses. The idea was exactly to do what colonists had done before, namely to make the governor dependent on the legislature, especially on its lower house. The number of years the executive could continue in office was usually limited. Rotation in office was often mandated. Franchise was expanded and the lower house elected by the people. What we do not see here is genuflection to any native national authority. "Nothing has excited more admiration in the world," James Madison wrote, "than the manner in which free governments have been established in America."[30]

No one, in my opinion, has effectively refuted the position taken by Claude Van Tyne in a 1907 article for the *American Historical Review*, which sought to show that the subjective idea of nationhood had not existed at the time. Of course, given the tools available, he is not able to show exactly that. But he is able to show the preeminent place of the states and gives many examples of state defiance of Continental Congress decisions. He shows that those men considered the best representatives were chosen to and chose themselves to serve the states.[31] Though it is true that the Continental Congress had some sort of navy, it was also true that nine of the thirteen states had navies of their own. The states did help organize the resistance to Britain, but states also organized armies of their own for their own purposes, whether or not this was useful for the common cause. If Congress had authorized the formation of states, it had also emphasized that this authority ran only during the war.[32] Although Congress undoubtedly exercised sovereign acts during that war, such as self defense, Virginia ratified a treaty with France, and South Carolina gave its government the right to make war and peace and to conclude treaties. Virtually everything the national government did, in a word, was done by many of the states. Against Irving Brant's stipulation of hundreds of statements of national consciousness,[33] Van Tyne earlier showed that specific acts indicated dominant state power.

Leaving aside the impulse for unity against a foreign foe, Greene sets out five conditions that limited expression and action of national sentiments: the considerable suspicion and mutual enmity among the colonies, the fear of a power-hungry central government, disbelief that a continental-size republic could endure, strong colonial identity as a distinct corporation "with an unquestioned commitment to preserve that identity," and "the primitive state of American national consciousness."

The View from Abroad

Before we turn to the efforts of American colonists to establish some sort of national government to carry on the war, it will be useful to visualize how arguments about sovereignty looked across the Atlantic to those who occupied the king's offices in Britain. What did

Americans mean, Edmund Morgan asked, "when they admitted due subordination to Parliament and at the same time denied Parliament's right to tax them?"[34] Soon enough colonials argued that they owed loyalty to the king but not to Parliament. What did that leave for Parliament? Presumably, Parliament might legislate for the entire British empire, though apparently not for any of its constituent parts. Not until 1931 was such a view of the empire as a commonwealth officially maintained.

In a well-known essay, Andrew McLaughlin argued that past practices under British rule actually embodied federal principles. For then the colonies almost entirely governed themselves. Were one to add "merely" the power of the central government to tax, McLaughlin claimed that government was federal in fact though not in form.[35] But what can be the federal element in a government described as did the freeholders of Granville County, North Carolina: "Resolved, That the executive power, constitutionally vested in the Crown and which presides equally over Great Britain and America, is a sufficient security for the due subordination of the Colonies without the Parliament's assuming powers of Legislation and Taxation which we enjoy distinct from, and in equal degree with them."[36] No doubt, as McLaughlin asserted, the old empire was a composite. But was it federal? My understanding is that a system in which the central government is dependent for supply upon the local or regional governments is a confederation, not a federal system. To put it the other way around, when the central government devolves powers upon local or regional governments, powers which it may take back, that is called a unitary and not a federal system.[37] In practice, the empire did little to assert its rule, and, when opposed, until the very end, it gave way. Then, in practice, I would say, it was a unitary government with a high degree of decentralization in which the central government gave what it thought necessary and the regional governments withheld whenever they could.[38]

Both victory and defeat have their problems. In victory, it is often hard to know whether to be grateful or fearful. At the end of the Seven Years' War, from 1756 to 1763, Great Britain emerged with an immense empire. From the French it had taken India and much of North America, and from the Spanish and French their commercial advantages. However, this victory committed the British to hold onto its conquests in the North American continent and to press ever further westward. How would it do so?[39] Always Britain was made hesitant by the fear that the French and perhaps the Spanish would take advantage of a war in North America.[40]

At the same time, "a look at the national debt in 1763," Robert Middlekauff tells us, "would have sent any minister's heart down into his shoes." The political limits of taxation within England had apparently been reached. Beer and cider taxes were hardly popular.[41] How surprising is it, in these circumstances, that Chancellor of the Exchequer Townshend proposed modest taxes. Together with public opinion in England and virtually all members of Parliament, he believed that actions intended to secure the defense of the colonies should be supported in part by their own revenues, and that Parliament had the right to impose them.[42]

There followed British efforts to tax a variety of commodities, all of which were resisted. The British insisted on the parliamentary right to impose taxes because, without that, they would lose such control over the colonies as they still exercised. Lord Mansfield claimed that the colonial position of denying sovereignty to Parliament and claiming attachment only to a king who, however, could not rule, was to make of the British monarch a "cypher." It would be a long time before the British monarch of the 1700s became converted into the constitutional monarch of today.[43] Tucker and Hendrickson argue that the conflict between the colonies and the king was intractable. It was not a case of misunderstanding one another but of having positions too contrary to be reconciled. Indeed, they deny the colonists' sentiment of attachment to Britain, asking of what did it consist if they were not willing to contribute to their own defense?[44] The one strategy that might have succeeded, had it been tried earlier, a strategy of sucking colonial elites into the vortex of government in the center of the empire itself so as "to channel their natural aspirations to an authority and status commensurate to their growing economic and social power" does not appear to have been considered.[45]

The Continental Congresses

Study of the First and Second Continental Congresses offers an extraordinary opportunity to observe a noncentralized government at work, albeit under adverse conditions. Whereas the Founding Fathers claimed to have devised a government by study and reflection, the founders of the Continental Congresses can make no such claim. Theirs was a spasm response. Faced with the British Parliament's Boston Port Act, which demanded indemnities for the tea lost by the East India Company (closing the facility until the demand was met), acts radically altering the government of Massachusetts, amending the Quartering Act so as to require putting up and providing for the empire's military, on and on, colonists soon realized they had to concert a response so as to achieve consensus in their opposition to rule by the British.[46] On the one hand, it is easy to spot many deficiencies in their jerry-built response; on the other hand, Congress did win the war. After describing what Congress did and did not do, I shall have a few words to say about how the centralized system of Great Britain handled the war. It will be fair to say that Congress did not do wonderfully, but Parliament and the king did worse.

The First Continental Congress quickly decided that each colony should have one and only one vote, though it did also insist that this not constitute a precedent. It lacked information about the wealth and population of each colony that might have provided some arithmetic mode of apportionment, and its members did not wish to engage in this sort of disputation faced with a common enemy. They acted, as might be expected, on the principle of achieving as much unity as possible, and one mode of achieving this end was not to discuss disputatious subjects.[47]

Even in 1774 and lasting into 1775, the instructions diverse colonies gave to their delegates included restoration of harmony and union with Britain. Several instructions were merely to attend the Congress and report back. Only North Carolina bound its delegates to accept whatever Congress decided. It is hard to make a plan of union out of typical instructions, such as those given to delegates in New Hampshire:

> To devise, consult, and adopt measures, as may have the most likely tendency to extricate the Colonies from their present difficulty; to secure and perpetuate their rights, liberties, and privileges, and to restore that peace, harmony, and mutual confidence which once happily subsisted between the parent country and her Colonies.[48]

Like the Stamp Act Congress that preceded it, the First Continental Congress was united by its opposition to the parliamentary acts, which is why it confined its proceedings to statements of its case and appeals for mitigation.[49]

A feeling for an assembly in which every man had not only a right but felt a duty to speak his mind is captured in John Adams' diary: "The business of Congress is tedious beyond expression. This assembly is like no other that ever existed. Every man in it . . . must show his oratory, his criticism and his political abilities." Consequently, meetings were interminable.[50] The Second Continental Congress, which met in 1775 and lasted throughout the Revolutionary War, was, not surprisingly, concerned over all with war. When the war went badly, it was consumed with ways and means of salvaging the effort; when the war went well, with some surprise Congress found itself dealing with other issues, including the form of government that would emerge after the war. As Congress surprised itself and its people by rapidly organizing the war effort, voices were heard urging a national union but of unspecified character.[51]

Within a week, Congress approved a request by Massachusetts to carry on with legal government. The collection and manufacture of ammunition provided occasion for a series of speedy recommendations. Soon enough there were resolutions forming a Continental Army. The next day George Washington was made commanding general, following by a plan for making staff appointments. The next week bills of credit were issued for the first time, and later that month there was issued a set of military regulations.[52]

The one item that seemed to cause controversy, strangely enough in retrospect, was George Washington's appointment. But this has much to teach us about sectional issues.[53] What on earth could have occasioned objection to the desire of New Englanders to appoint George Washington commander in chief in June of 1775? Evidently, they thought that recommending a Southerner would enhance national unity. But Southerners were fearful that they might suffer at the hands of a senior army staff dominated by Northerners. At the beginning, only three of fourteen senior officers were from the South. Congress overruled seniority in order to prevent domination of the army by Northern officers. Jibes to the effect that Massachusetts men make good soldiers but Southerners better officers did not help.[54]

For their own part, the New Englanders envisioned the war fought by citizen generals in command of volunteer local militias who enlisted for relatively short periods and were free to withdraw at almost any time. Private benefits as a motive were anathema compared to moral fervor. The slavery of the South did not seem virtuous to them.

How might a republic based on citizen virtue be created there under such conditions?[55] The Southerners feared a strong national government directed by people who looked down on them and who might interfere with their plans for extending their way of life to the west.[56]

By 1780, after many frustrations, Congress moved toward a more efficient mode of administration. Instead of debating and discussing matters large and, alas, small in infinite tedium, Congress began to create executive departments. The numerous boards and commissions to deal with every subject under the sun were rationalized and placed under the supervision of department heads responsible to Congress. It devoted less time to trying individual cases of malfeasance or corruption. The hope was that the previous rapid change in administrative appointments would slow down and lead to more responsive and responsible administration.[57] Self-interest was given greater reign. Efforts were made to create and nurture allies abroad rather than rely on republican virtue alone at home. A professional military was to be created with conventional, that is, material, rewards. And the self-denial of patriots was supplemented by the self-regard of businessmen.[58]

It would have been better for Congress to pay commissaries, that is, purchasing agents, high salaries and attempt to keep them honest. But Congress initially thought otherwise. It denied the commissaries regular commissions, which might have substituted status for income; it demanded elaborate records, including not only the number but the birthmarks of cattle and, in an excess of frugality, it paid below-market prices for wagons and supply trains, a practice not appreciated by owners who found more lucrative trade.[59] Even when Congress decided to divide the functions into a commissary of purchases and one of provisions, problems of supply did not end. Congress felt that individuals should not profit from the war. Thus they rejected the practice of giving a commission of 1–1/2 percent of the value of all supplies, a provision that had the effect of encouraging considerable activity on the part of the agents.[60] Quartermasters themselves did work on a commission basis and generally performed ably, even if partly for themselves.[61]

It should be understood that throughout history military officers have demonstrated high-handed ways, including taking whatever they needed wherever they found it without regard to proper procedure. The supply sergeant of modern lore who can find nearly anything is one such individual, much appreciated, at least in American movies, but little understood. Back then, looting of supply trains was a normal condition.[62] The problems of supply were, in any case, difficult. How were Southern products to get to Northern armies? One of Robert Morris's contributions was the policy of selling supplies contributed in the South so they could be purchased nearer where the armies were fighting in the North.[63]

It was not long before questions of national versus state authority came up through the mechanism of decisions about how to carry on the war. How about the apprehension of deserters? Could Congress, acting solely on its own authority, direct local agencies to capture deserters? Was James Wilson right in arguing that there was an implicit authority in Congress to deal with matters of continental-wide concern? Such arguments represented American rephrasing of the British claim that Parliament had sovereignty over empire-wide matters that it alone could define. Was Thomas Burke right in protesting that legitimating this use of coercive authority would alter the form of government?[64]

In the midst of a rather difficult and demanding debate about the regulation of prices, a larger question supervened: should Congress give its approval to a meeting of four New England states to discuss this matter? Given that the subject of price regulation was continental in scope, Benjamin Rush argued they should not have met at all without congressional approval. In the end, Congress decided not to decide by stipulating that, under prevailing conditions, the meeting was all right.[65]

Failure in supply is now, as it was then, the crucial complaint levied against the Continental Congress. For it raised the key question of whether the national entity had the right and the ability to levy taxes directly on citizens without going through the states. This was no small matter, representing the difference between a national and a confederal government.

Washington fought a defensive war. His aim was not so much to secure victories as to avoid defeats, and if defeat was inevitable, to retreat. Washington and his army did suffer defeats, but they also learned and survived. The major difficulties they encountered, aside from the sting of defeat and melting away of troops, came from insufficient supply and pay. A defensive war had certain advantages when the defenders knew the terrain and had the support of local people. But it did depend crucially on supply.

The Impost

Financing large-scale war has never been easy. It was not easy for Great Britain during the Revolutionary War. It was doubly difficult for thirteen separate colonies whose financial capacities and financial administration were far from brilliant. Before going into the grave difficulties the Continental Congress faced in attempting to finance the war, it is essential to understand the conditions of the time. The war produced episodic fluctuations in revenue and expenditure for the states. The lore on which taxes might produce the most revenue in the fastest period of time, state by state, was underdeveloped. Who could say which type of tax would serve the purpose while stirring the least political opposition, and who could say what those taxes were, state by state, given the considerable disparities among them? If to these uncertainties one were to add the difficulties of apportioning the burden among the states, it is no wonder Congress faced horrendous difficulties. Were colonies to resist British taxation only to impose much heavier burdens upon themselves, not from their own legislatures, but from a distant Congress? No wonder everyone's first thought was to leave it to the states to figure out what sort of taxes would best suit their conditions.[66]

The system Congress first adopted was expedient: it made requisitions upon states and hoped they would supply the funds. The common cause aided in this effort. But there were also interests dividing the states. Higher taxes in one state might mean that citizens would move to another or to the frontier. Each state had an interest in keeping its taxes low. How could the disparate abilities of the states to pay, including their greatly varying populations, be made compatible with policies that would not disadvantage one compared to the others?

The heart of the problem, Tucker and Hendrickson rightly tell us, "lay in the tendency of the requisition system to depress the contributions of the participants to the lowest common denominator. It made the action of the least zealous the effective standard for the action of all."[67]

When we realize that in 1781 Congress requisitioned $8 million for the next fiscal year but the states paid less than half a million, the size of the problem becomes apparent. During the entire period under the Articles of Confederation, "the cumulative amount paid by all the states hardly exceeded what was required to pay the interest on the public debt for just one year."[68] Reports on unmet needs of the army prepared during the autumn of 1780 and the winter of 1781 resulted in two major recommendations. One, passed on February 3, 1781, requested states to enable Congress to collect a duty (an impost) on foreign goods to the end that the confederation might at long last obtain an independent source of revenue. Adopted a few days later, the second created three executive departments—War, Marine, and Finance—to add to the previously-approved Department of Foreign Affairs. Until his departure in 1783, Robert Morris became the head of finance.[69]

Approval of the impost under the existing form of government required an amendment to the Articles. In the end, all the states but Rhode Island ratified the impost. But under the unanimity rule for amendments to the Articles, the impost was defeated.

Congress might try to negotiate treaties to protect American shipping, but it was quite another matter to have the states ratify them. An amendment authorizing an embargo against ships of nations which had not signed a treaty with the United States was ratified by only four states.[70]

It was not long before the impost became converted from an ameliorative measure to meet immediate needs to a question of who had the power to do what. No one doubted the desirability of raising revenue. As Congress debated the matter, the text changed from its confederal form—asking states individually to pass statutes enabling them to collect the impost to pass along to Congress—and became instead a request to the states to vest this power in Congress. Moreover, the purpose for which the revenue was to be spent was narrowed to one of reducing the interest and principal on the national debt.[71]

Before leaping to conclusions, it would be well to consider Rakove's considered judgment "that any different result would have occurred had Congress rather than the states been vested with the power of taxation."[72] It is one thing to cry out against the inability to support the war and soldiers' pay, and another to claim that had Congress been given that power it would have been more successful than the states in collecting the money. Mann writes in accord with observation of the time that had Congress allowed the revenues collected to be credited to the colony in which the goods were consumed, as well as collection by state officers, the measures would have been approved.[73] But then there could have been no guarantees that Congress would have received the funds or even that they would have been applied to the conduct of war. State governments might have considered retaining public support more important than reducing the debt.

Burdened and frustrated by Congress's inability to collect revenues, Robert Morris let it be widely known that he would resign unless things improved. This angered many without furthering his cause. Just when it appeared that financial matters would get even worse, the Articles of Peace containing the British surrender, appeared as a sign of happier days to come.[74] An interesting sidelight to the story is provided by the fact that, after Morris left office in 1784, he was succeeded on the Board of Treasury by republican-minded delegates, Richard Henry Lee and Samuel Osgood, who came full of belief that honesty and frugality would conquer all. With prospects of selling Western lands, they as well as others thought the debt might soon be extinguished. As life would have it, however, within a couple of years they were writing nasty letters about feckless and unreliable states much in the style of Morris.[75]

The war was over, it had been won, and both Congress and states were left with debts for their pains. The presenting problem was the demobilization of the army, much of which had not been paid or paid too little or with certificates whose value was uncertain. But for Washington's intervention, the situation might have become nasty. In the event, the army followed his lead and returned to the plough.[76] By then, however, tired of narrow scrapes and feelings of impotence, the nationalists in the colonies who had once hoped to rejoin the British now saw they could make a strong case for a national government.

The Unitary State at War

The advantages of a unitary state at war lie in its ability to raise resources, maintain armies and navies, and concert force. These advantages depend on certain assumptions that are not usually unearthed. One of these is that revenue raising is painless or not sufficiently painful to cause resistance. Another is that there is in fact, as well as in form, unity of direction at the top. If, by contrast, its governments are internally divided, their will weak or aimless, and their capacity to suffer adversity small, all of which conditions were met in the British empire, these advantages turn into dust. It is true that the criticism unleashed in a noncentralized system may inhibit action and delay worthwhile remedies. It is also true that lack of criticism, at least in public, may permit evils to go on far longer in unitary governments than in those polities where harms are more readily brought to light.

In addition to the advantages brought by its large size and, according to the norms of the times, its considerable military prowess, the British empire faced a number of disadvantages in dealing with unruly colonials. The North American continent was far away, thereby creating severe problems of supply. Great Britain's military strategy depended on control of the seas, a control that could be fragile were the French and/or Spanish to intervene in force. Its homeland was not threatened, whereas the colonials' was. This meant that colonials were likely to fight more fiercely and to be willing to endure more sacrifice than those for whom the difficulties were remote. With responsibilities in India and in other points around the globe, furthermore, the British government could hardly be insensitive to how developments in one part of the world might affect its position in the others.[77]

What were its objectives in regard to the colonists? Was it to beat down the rebellion so that the empire's ties to the colonies might be reinstated as they were of old? Was it to defeat them decisively so as to establish a British government over a subject population? Was it to put American royalists in power?[78] The British could not decide, perhaps because they thought there was no need to decide until they had subdued the colonists' will to fight on.

To say that there was a government in Parliament was not to say that it commanded a decisive majority on all questions or even necessarily on any single one, apart from its retention in office. Lord North ministry's majority was slim and subject to dissipation. Nor would the king provide whatever leadership was necessary. He would jolly up the ministers and tell them to hang together, but he would not or could not tell them what to do. In that case, no failure in policy could unseat the king. By the same token, telling ministers to put more steel in their spines was not quite the same as telling them in what direction to aim it.[79]

The British part in the Revolutionary War was a classic case of administrative inefficiency. In its time, this was par for the course, but it hurt especially far from home where supply lines were long and cries for attention unheard. Behemoths may roll over opposition, but they are not easily bestirred. Though the rebellion was long seen to be coming, little was done except to dispatch a few regiments. To do more, the cabinet would have had to face up to the fact that it needed a much larger army and therefore much more money.[80]

Patronage was rife. By great good fortune, a patron might have recommended someone with talent and energy, but that was not the usual case. Consequently, British officers did not have to depend on their superiors but on those who appointed them, discipline was lax and inefficiency rampant. For instance, out of six people appointed as commissaries, whose performance was vital to the war, only one had previous experience. One had as his chief qualification that he had been an acquaintance of Lord North, others that they were loyalists who preyed on the king's sympathy. A man with the right connections, despite complaints, might be appointed to one position, dismissed for incompetence, and then appointed to a similar position elsewhere.[81]

Added to patronage was amateurism, the belief that any generalist could do any task. Disaster soon followed. Even worse, perhaps, was the effort to slough off responsibility on others or on no one in particular. When it became known that subordinates would be held to task if they took unauthorized actions, it became commonplace to demand justification in cabinet minutes before actions could be undertaken.[82] Yet without taking action on the spot, the cause in America would be lost.

During the first four years of the war, provisions were supplied through the Treasury. This was a grave error as that department was in no way prepared for the task. Its officials didn't know the business and, worse perhaps, many did not care to know. There were neither proper warehouses nor accounts.[83] Only when the navy (which knew what it was doing, more or less) took over supplies did the situation begin to improve.

Often supply ships were delayed. Always those who sent them made no allowance for delay. Often ships were sent without adequate consideration for facilities for unloading and transport to wherever armies were.[84] General Pattison wrote to his superiors in a despairing, half-mocking tone: "I presume if we are to continue here it is not intended to be in a state of nakedness."[85] General Clinton had General Dalrymple sail back home complaining that "we have no small arms and are so much in want of powder that I scarcely dare fire a salute or permit the troops to practice."[86]

The lack of supplies was particularly unfortunate because it helped prevent the British from undoing Washington's strategy by seeking decisive battles. When an army has to live off the land, it cannot pursue and fight but must go wherever it can provision itself.[87]

Mackesy gives us an odyssey of shipping problems. Here was a force of supply ships ready to sail on the first of December. Alas, the Ordinance Department could not supply the necessary guns and munitions so the ship was delayed for two weeks. Another two weeks were spent fighting adverse winds, so the ships were more or less back where they started. Another week was lost in getting to Ireland, so what with one thing and another, the flotilla did not set sail until February 12. When the ships finally did get under way, General Howe wrote to call off the expedition.[88]

Of course, one hand did not know very much about what the other was doing, especially when that hand was 3,000 miles away. Thus did the Treasury discover that in some short period of time the army had consumed 3–1/2 million pounds more of bread and flour and 2 million pounds more of meat than had been expected. One reason supplies ran short was that far away in England there was no knowledge of thousands of extra mouths to feed, including prisoners of war, Indians, relatives and camp followers.[89]

A few words about General Burgoyne's transport problems should complete the picture. Though he ordered officers to reduce their baggage to minimum proportions, his orders were not obeyed. It was not just a few but many officers who found it advantageous to acquire more horses and even wagons for themselves, as the fortunes of war provided. The king's carts, as they were called, often fell into the wrong hands, albeit supposedly on one's own side.[90] Though Burgoyne issued orders to hire all the wagons his people could find, and he assumed they could find them, they either were not available or the officers were derelict in their duty. Nor were the local people friendly and disposed to give aid and comfort.[91] Tacticians may differ over whether Burgoyne demanded the transport of too many big guns. Nevertheless, as Bowler puts it, "the artillery employed 400 horses that not only ate up large parts of the supply of hay and oats, but might have been used to carry provisions or even to mount the German Dragoons."[92] For mercy's sake, I omit mention of the many times ships sailed into the wrong ports.[93]

Daring and resolve were not necessarily qualities sought or found in British high command. Its generalship was poor, and it hesitated or, when more daring, failed to get sufficient support. A security- and seniority-oriented army, whose name at the top was Patronage, was not suited to wars far away. Whatever happened, they could always return to their privileged life. No British general ever outlined a plan designed to bring victory. They fought catch-as-catch-can, some better, some worse, until loss of naval support at Yorktown and a general wearing down of their armies compelled them to submit.

There is no way of knowing whether the inconveniences and inefficiencies of a noncentralized form of government were equal to, lesser than, or greater than those that attended the prosecution of the war in America by Great Britain. What seems reasonable to say is that, given considerable inefficiency on both sides, those committed by the British had worse effects on their military position than those that afflicted George Washington's armies, which experienced better treatment at the hands of local populations.

Republican Egalitarian Ideology

Before we can understand the debates about either the Articles of Confederation or the Constitution, it is necessary to know something about the republican ideology of the period. Thinking of the struggles in England between what was called the Party of the Country versus the Party of the King over whether the monarch's patronage would undermine representative government, the radical part of the Whig opposition, sometimes called republican, put forward ideas that found only modest resonance within England but a ready audience among American political activists. The most important things to know about this ideology, in my opinion, are that it was strongly egalitarian and that its adherents believed that the national government (as distinguished from state and local governments) was a feared source of artificial inequality. By artificial they meant inequalities not inherent in human character and talent but imposed by governmental action in providing privileges to some citizens that were denied to others.[94] Though equality in the sense of social leavening, Wood informs us, was not seriously conceived of in 1776, there were adherents of reducing what they called unnecessary and unwarranted distinctions. As suited their purposes, they were ambiguous in their thought in refusing to distinguish between equal opportunity and equal conditions. On one side, according to Wood, their doctrine "stressed equality of opportunity which implied social differences and distinctions; on the other . . . it emphasized equality of condition which denied these same social differences and distinctions."[95] What the Whig opposition and their American followers meant by what "Cato" called "a relatively equal division of property" cannot be accurately stated. But there was a wider agreement that a country like the United States, where property was fairly widely distributed compared to the usual European condition, had a better chance of forming a representative government.[96]

Mann quotes the writer called "Democritus" who warned that "only those could be trusted who earned their living by 'honest industry' and who were men 'in middling circumstances.'"[97] Who can fault here the egalitarian protests of the people of Farmington:

> Because it is founded on Principles Subertive of a Republican Government Tending to Destroy that Equality among the citisans which [is] the only permanent foundation on which it can be supported to throw an excessive Power, the constant attendent of property into the Hands of the Few, to cherish those anti-republican Principles & feelings which are now predominant in many of the states, and finally to dissolve our present Happy and Benevolent Constitution & to erect on the Ruins, a proper Aristocracy: wherein the Body of the People are excluded from all share in the Government, and the Direction & management of the state is committed to the Great & Powerful alone.[98]

I follow Wood in his important summary: "The republican aversion to artificial distinctions was being broadened into a general denunciation of all differences, whether economic, social, intellectual, or professional."[99]

In sum, the Whig ideology saw two great threats to liberty, one the moral decay of a people that ought to be dedicated to public virtue and disinterestedness and instead became corrupted by wealth and unmerited distinction, "and the encroachment of executive authority upon the legislature, the attempt that power always made to subdue the liberty protected by mixed government."[100] One need only connect these sentiments to those of a man of Whiggish bent from Delaware who claimed that "the executive power is ever restless, ambitious, and ever grasping an encrease of power" to understand the republican desire for legislative supremacy.[101] The repeated calls for separation of powers may be interpreted, as Banning does, as "essentially a demand for an end to executive influence upon and interference with the other branches of government."[102] They feared that inequality within government would surely lead to the destruction of republican government as inequality in society. The Articles of Confederation was a republican construct.

The Articles of Confederation

"Throughout the 1770's," Wood informs us, "there was remarkably little discussion in the press or pamphlets of the nature of the union being formed. What debate there was . . . was very limited and intellectually insignificant in comparison with the exciting and sweeping debates over the formation of the state constitutions—a graphic indication of the relative importance Americans attributed to their central and state governments."[103]

Had there been no sentiment for a national entity in addition to states, there would have been no Articles of Confederation. A unitary state was out of the question. Could there, however, have been a federal state with both national and state governments exercising direct authority over citizens as provided for in the Constitution? Though not directly discussed as such, the idea of a national government did come up and was explicitly rejected in favor of a confederate form of government.

The short life of the Articles of Confederation began in March 1781, though the drafting took place in the years 1776 and 1777. It was over by 1789 when the Constitution came into force. The very fact that there was virtually no opposition to the Constitution after it began tells us that its principles cannot have been considered outrageous by many. It would be equally valid to say that, until then, the idea of dual sovereignty had very little currency in the United States.

In 1780 and 1781 a number of amendments to the Articles were considered with the idea of giving Congress an independent source of revenue, as we saw in discussing the impost. The impost failed because of the unanimity requirement, which may well be regarded the single and most signal failure of government under that document. There was widespread agreement that the Articles needed improvement but, when faced with the stark choice of no improvement or radical change, change—what we now call the American federal system—won out. I shall end this paper with brief speculations about how life under the Articles might have developed had sufficient change been made to increase the efficacy of that confederal government. Here, before we examine how well governments and peoples fared while living under a noncentralized form of government, we must attend to the actual provisions of the Articles.

On one side stood those like John Adams who believed that "the Confederacy is to make of us one individual only; is to form us like separate parcels of metal, into one common mass. We shall no longer retain our separate individuality, but become a single individual as to all questions submitted to the Confederacy." On the other side, people like Roger Sherman and John Witherspoon argued that such matters relating only to individuals neither could nor should come before the Congress, there was no need of a union to incorporate the states into one. Stephen Hopkins contended that "the Safety of the whole depends on the distinctions of Colonies."[104] The vital difference was that one side saw the defect of the Articles as its incapacity to act on individuals, and the other side saw that very same thing as protective of liberty.[105]

Everyone at the time understood, Merrill Jensen asserted, "that most of the state governments would never knowingly accept a superior government over them."[106] He is certainly accurate in pointing out that radicals of the Whig-republican persuasion in the eighteenth century "looked upon the desire for office as a disease which fed upon office-holding."[107] Such views were clearly written into the Articles: delegates were selected by state governments that could recall them at any time; the presidency of the Congress could be held by the same person no longer than one year out of three; nor could (*pace* term limits nowadays) a member of Congress serve for more than three years of the six-year term. Zuckert concludes that "the delegates were agents of, appointed by, sent to serve at the pleasure of, and paid by their states."[108]

The issue was joined in the difference between John Dickinson's draft of the Articles and the successful amendment, which became Article II, offered by Thomas A. Burke of North Carolina.

Dickinson:

> Each Colony shall retain and enjoy as much of its present Laws, Rights and Customs, as it may think fit, and reserves to itself the sole and exclusive Regulation and Government of its internal police, in all matters that shall not interfere with the Articles of Confederation.[109]

Burke:

Each State retains its sovereignty, freedom, and independence, and every power, jurisdiction, and right, which is not by this confederation expressly delegated to the United States, in Congress assembled.[110]

Dickinson's prohibition of states interfering with the government of the Articles was rejected. The phrase "expressly delegated to the United States" became in the Constitution the "necessary and proper" clause, a world of difference.

An Irish immigrant, with virtually no political past and not much of a future, Burke regarded his role entirely as a servant of his state and, in that capacity, kept a barely willing governor informed daily of events.[111] Essentially, Burke argued "That the states alone had Power to act coercively against their citizens, and therefore were the only Power competent to carry into execution any Provisions whether Continental or Municipal." Thus he got John Adams, among others, to admit that, if a declaration of war were to have effect, the "Articles of War must be enacted into Laws in the several States."[112] It is worth hearing what Rakove has to say:

With these qualifications, it is nevertheless unquestionable that Burke made a critical contribution to the evolution of American notions of confederation. He was the first to ask how conventional ideas of sovereignty were to be reconciled with the establishment of a confederation. And once this question, hitherto surprisingly ignored, was posed, there could be little doubt that the states were a more appropriate repository for sovereignty than was the union. The states were the constituent parties of the union: they elected and instructed the members of Congress, and their consent was indisputably necessary for the ratification of confederation. The states possessed governments constructed in the normal meaning of the term, exercising legislative, executive, and judicial functions, while Congress remained, so to speak, structurally anomalous.[113]

The first three Articles created "a firm league of friendship" for the security and general welfare of the states. The fourth promised to end various discriminatory actions of one state against another, allowed for the extradition of fugitives, and contained a clause adopted by the Constitution that "the Citizens of each State shall be entitled to all Privileges and Immunities of Citizens in the several States." Whether, as Lutz argues, this was tantamount to acceptance of dual sovereignty in that each individual was simultaneously a citizen of a state and of the nation is an open question.[114]

In addition to the conditions of appointment of delegates from the states we have already discussed, Article V stated that "Each state shall maintain its own delegates in a meeting of the states, and while they act as members of the committee of the states."[115] A clearer statement of state supremacy could hardly be given. The most national of the Articles, VI, held that states were prohibited from making alliances or treaties with other governments or entering into such between any two states or keeping war vessels without congressional consent or engaging in war or contravening treaties "entered into by the United States and Congress."[116] Articles VII and VIII held that expenses of war for the common defense should be determined by the land within each state as well as the improvements on it. But "the taxes for paying that proportion shall be laid and levied by the authority and direction of the legislatures of the several states within a time agreed upon by the United States in Congress assembled."[117] What was to be done should the states fail to pay was not discussed.

The ninth Article provides an elaborate procedure for dealing with disputes among the states and makes clear again that foreign policy and war belongs to Congress. The rest of the Articles allow Canada but no other entity to enter the Confederation, and that nine of the thirteen states shall be sufficient to pass ordinary laws.

Ratification of the Articles of Confederation was held up for three years due to Maryland's refusal to ratify. A number of its leading citizens held title to lands that were variously claimed by Virginia and New York. Only when these two states recognized they could not acceptably govern the vast tracts of land they claimed, and ceded them to a national domain in return for clearer title to lands they still held, was Maryland persuaded to sign on March 1, 1781.[118]

The Articles of Confederation sought to draw a line between internal and external affairs. In regard to internal matters, states were sovereign and Congress could act only through them. In foreign affairs, however, Congress, composed of a committee of the states, held a ruling hand, though how it might enforce its will on the states remained unstated. The states retained their internal police powers while Congress hoped that in matters of war and peace and foreign affairs, as well as those unspecified of a continental character, the whole would prevail over the parts. This is largely a confederal, not a federal, government.

No wonder that men who sought power and distinction would rather serve in their states than in the Congress. No wonder that much time was consumed in fruitless quorum calls as seven states were required to be in attendance. No wonder that proceedings were stymied when certain delegates were absent and when their views were opposed so that their state vote did not count.[119] It would appear that nothing good could come of this. But it did. The claims of the nationalists of the day that trade was Balkanized, that states made economic war on each other, that debtors seized control of state legislatures and inflated the currency—in short, that anarchy reigned, as exemplified by Shay's Rebellion—was well publicized at the time and continues to this day. Historians reexamining these episodes, however, have come to contrary or at least to mixed conclusions. Let us turn now to experience.

Life under the Articles

It is now too late, and records kept at the time are too scanty, to arrive at definitive conclusions about the nature of the American economy during the period of the Articles. There is no doubt that during the scant few years under the Articles there were economic difficulties. How could there not be? Commerce had been disrupted and resources diverted into the Revolutionary War. It would take some time to build up the productive capacity of the economy. A recession, judged by economists to be of a cyclical kind, occurred at more or less the same time; and the colonies no longer had what today we would call imperial preferences. But there was also a brighter side. Self reliance during the war led to an increase in domestic manufactures. Trade with European nations other than Britain increased.[120] Exports increased moderately, prices generally were higher, and the condition of the people, when reported upon, generally appeared good.[121] Whether the substantial increase in tonnage on American ships as well as the increase in exports reflected merely the considerable growth in population or increased economic growth remains in doubt.[122] No one in those days imagined the positive effects on trade of the Napoleonic wars or on manufacturing of Eli Whitney's invention of the cotton gin. It is also worth noting that there was a considerable base in terms of resources and human talent for commerce before the Revolutionary War.[123] What we can say is that the picture of a prostrate America caused by the absence of strong central government is overdrawn.

Readers of the Federalist Papers will recognize the many complaints against interference with commerce in the form of special burdens placed by one state on another. They will also recall, if pressed, that the matter is not discussed in any depth or detail but rather assumed. Certain background factors, as usual, will be helpful in guiding interpretation.

Except for tobacco and cotton, most commerce occurred not between states, given the primitive transportation modes of the day, but rather from the export of raw materials to Europe and the import of finished goods and manufactures. Trade from individual states to Europe and back was the largest kind. What is today called interstate commerce was relatively small.[124]

It will be helpful to consider the general objectives to which tariffs and regulations were directed. One was revenue, another was protection of local industries, and a third was retaliation against other states and nations.[125]

One of the common allegations of the time was that states having ports where goods would be unloaded would raise fees and other obstacles to their shipment to the states for which they were intended. The most egregious case was New York's duty on imports destined for other states.[126] But a study of that provision discovered that, upon submission of a sworn statement that these goods were destined for individuals in other states, they passed duty free, though they did have to be sent in the same package though not the same vessel. This was a common feature of policy throughout the states.[127] There were also a number of small quarrels that led to a round of retaliations from one state to another, but they were cleared up by new legislation. The nub of the difficulty was that New York and Massachusetts wanted to discriminate against British goods in retaliation for the Navigation Acts. The amounts involved were small and, after some haggling, the difficulties resolved.[128]

In a study of tariff policies in Virginia, which occasioned much criticism at the time, William Zornow shows that an act of 1788 provided that virtually all goods produced in the United States were able to enter Virginia duty-free. Criticisms that had been true up to that time were no longer correct.[129] Virginians had never been afforded special tariff rates unavailable to other American citizens. By the time the government under the Constitution assumed office, there was very nearly free trade.[130] There were, of course, protective tariffs in Virginia, but that was as common then for states as it is now for nations.[131] In a further study of Massachusetts tariff legislation in practice, Zornow explains that at no time were American goods from other states discriminated against. By 1789, the trend was entirely toward free trade among the United States, and increasingly greater efforts were made to bring policies in one state in accord with others.[132]

Experience in South Carolina reveals a strong tendency to discriminate against foreigners, a weaker but still palpable tendency to discriminate against residents of other states, and a growing tendency toward freer trade. Whether one chooses to focus on the discriminatory policies or on the tendency to move away from them is a matter of judgment. To place South Carolina's policies in perspective, it is necessary to understand that many states sought to regulate economic activities in a way they believed would be favorable to their interests. Thus, South Carolina gave bounties (now called subsidies) for those who would make flour out of wheat, grow hemp and flax, and manufacture thread or saleable linens. This practice died after the Revolutionary War. It was replaced by tariffs against the importation of these very same materials and manufactures. Duties of all kinds against non-American citizens were common. In the midst of such regulatory policies, South Carolina caused modest harm and considerable outrage in other states by placing duties on goods in transit to American locations and placing duties on tonnage of American but not South Carolinian ships.[133] In addition, there were numerous small but cumulatively burdensome charges for lighthouses, hospitals, storage, pilotage and tonnage for non-South Carolinian ships. This sort of thing made the charges levied by Tenche Coxe of Pennsylvania (and picked up by nationalists of all kinds) seem valid. Looked at over time, however, the trend was toward freer trade. South Carolina went along with efforts of the Congress to impose uniform duties. Tariffs and charges against goods from other American states were gradually reduced, and were nearly eliminated by the time the Constitution came into force.[134]

A government with the power to control interstate commerce undoubtedly would have suffered fewer of these difficulties. But this is not to say that a noncentralized system could not have evolved in a similar direction and was not, in fact, in process of doing so. Were the inconveniences of the period from the end of the Revolutionary War through 1789 serious enough to condemn government under the Articles? I think not. Opposite breaches in modern times, which allow the central government to regulate commerce wholly within a single state on the grounds that it places a burden on interstate commerce, might not have taken place.

Shay's Rebellion

Was George Washington right when he wrote Richard Henry Lee that "to be more exposed in the eyes of the world and more contemptible than we already are, is hardly possible" or when he told James Madison that "we are fast verging to anarchy and confusion."? Was Lee in turn in touch with the situation when he asserted that "we are all in dire apprehension that a beginning of anarchy with all its calamities is approached, and have no means to stop the dreadful work"? John Jay wrote Thomas Jefferson that he smelled more than a redress of grievances in the Shayites.[135]

In the spring and summer of 1786 courts charged with the duty of collecting debts were forcibly shut down in a number of localities in Massachusetts. The government of Massachusetts, its General Court, refused to accede to the twin demands of relief from debt and lower taxes. When the rebellion grew, government offered the carrot of an amnesty together with the stick of raising an army. Early in 1787 Shay and his followers were routed; the leaders left the state, the followers went home. A small occupying army was stationed in the areas of greatest rebellion and court officers were empowered to collect what was due.[136]

Whereas the use of force to put down the rebellion had widespread support, the occupying army and its minions did not. Increasing calls came for lenient governmental policy. From being a traitor to law and order, Daniel Shay "quickly became an object of pathos," especially when he went around begging for financial support. Had a lenient policy not been followed, it is possible that the anti-federalist fervor stemming from the repression of Shay's rebellion might have succeeded in getting Massachusetts to reject the Constitution.[137] Were one to compare Shay's rebellion with the Whiskey Rebellion that occurred during the presidency of George Washington, which was put down by the mobilization of an army greater than that which fought the Revolutionary War and ended in the temporary imprisonment of very few people, it would be hard to say which form of government was more vigorous in putting down this refusal to obey the law. It is possible to conclude that there was a lot less to these rebellions than there seemed to be.

Western Lands

Among the many difficulties faced in trying to govern diverse peoples recently emerged from a revolutionary war, with many ups and downs, the signal success of the Articles was its engineering of a land policy to which all the states would adhere. This was one problem the government under the new Constitution would not have to inherit. The key to settling this question lay in Virginia's cession of its claims under the old royal charter for immense tracts of land north of the Ohio River. Around the same time (March 1784) Congress passed the first ordinance on western lands that provided for self-government in these territories. Observing rather barbaric tactics in the territories, Congress adopted another ordinance in May 1785 dividing the land into townships six miles square. First the land was to be surveyed and then it was to be sold at not less than a dollar an acre, with governmental certificates accepted as specie. As each township was divided into thirty-six lots, lot sixteen in each town was reserved for public schools, and other land was to be used to pay off bounties promised soldiers during the Revolutionary War. As for the Confederation, it received one-third of all silver, gold, and copper discovered and four sections in each town.[138]

Thomas Jefferson played a large part in arranging these matters. He served on the committee of Congress which was placed in charge of devising policy for the western lands. His desire was virtually to give away the land so that it could be settled by small farmers, the sturdy yeomanry he so much admired. Give-aways, however, had little appeal when the public debt seemed so large and land was reserved for paying up its principal as Congress might decide. Jefferson's idea did succeed with the new states that would be formed out of the new territories and would be able to enter the union under the same conditions as the original thirteen.[139]

The greatest of all these acts, the Ordinance of 1787, later called the Northwest Ordinance, was passed on July 13, 1787. Territories were to be administered by a governor, a secretary, and three judges who were appointed by Congress. After there were 5,000 free inhabitants in that territory, they might create a general assembly to consist of a house of representatives, a legislative council, and the governor. The Ordinance also specified relatively easy rules for the admission of new states into the union. It represented a great act of statesmanship.

Sinking the Debt

Among the numerous accusations leveled at the government under the Articles of Confederation, the failure to sink (that is, retire) the debt was foremost. In significant measure, this was an unfair accusation. From the earliest times, the settlers of the united colonies suffered from a lack of specie, hard coin in which to conduct their transactions. With so little money in supply, it became easy to acquire debt and difficult to pay it off. By the time a farmer bought land and equipment, the sum was too high to be paid for out of savings and required going into debt. When anything went wrong, farmers found themselves unable to pay and at risk of losing their land. Debtor prisons were a growing industry. And debtors' riots became common.[140]

Debts connected farmers to politics. To get at one aspect of the problem, they sought to keep expenses and salaries in government very low so as to pay less in taxes. They also sought the issue of paper money, the deferment of charges, the levying of taxes payable with securities rather than specie, and the payment of interest in paper money.[141] Common practice in states was to issue paper money which was then withdrawn from circulation via proceeds from taxation. This was called "currency finance." The whole point was to get around the need for specie. "For over half a century before the Revolution," Ferguson observes, "colonial governments regularly issued and withdrew paper money, alternately creating and redeeming public debt."[142]

It would help the reader also to know that during the war Congress sold a kind of bond called "loan office certificates," worth about $11.5 million in species. Presumably they were held for individuals who had performed some special service in loaning money to Congress. Yet more complicated, interest was paid on face value though certificates were bought with depreciating currency and the interest was paid in what were called "bills of exchange" drawn on banks in France. These bills were especially valuable because they could be redeemed in specie. Interest rates ran as high as 25 percent. These certificates were often given to merchants in lieu of cash, and therefore came to be held by people of means. These loan office certificates were often referred to as public debt.

In addition to debt being a threat to the viability of the American union, it was also looked upon as an aid to that very union. Holding debt would give people of property a stake in the success of the new government. Moreover, and perhaps most important, according to Ferguson, "Congress intended to use the debt for a political purpose. Payment on the terms Congress proposed involved a grant of taxing power to the central government."[143]

It is fair to say that the picture passed down through the generations and perpetuated in our time is one of Congress struggling to pay off the public debt but not succeeding due to improvident and unwilling state legislatures. Not quite. Most of the some $200 million issued in paper money by states depreciated over time so that it was essentially wiped out. In an effort to straighten out these finances, Congress revalued the currency so that one unit of specie equaled 40 units of currency, and asked the states to withdraw the paper from circulation. Nearly $120 million was withdrawn. By 1790 it was estimated that only $6 million in certificates or $60,000 in specie remained in circulation, not a small but certainly not an overwhelming amount of debt.[144]

During the war the revolutionary armies, receiving so little from the Continental Congress, lived off the land. Mostly they were decent about it, giving merchants and farmers certificates. Estimates of the total value range over $100 million, but nobody knew for sure. In any event, Congress asked the states to accept these certificates in lieu of payment of taxes. Northern states redeemed part of them, and in the South, where they grew largest, state governments accepted them as equivalent to state debt and arranged to pay them off.[145]

There were also arrears in pay due to soldiers who fought in the Continental army. Several years of pay amounted to millions of dollars, especially considering that some soldiers enlisted for three years or the entire length of the war. Not only was there failure to pay these salaries at all, but payment was sometimes given in depreciated currency that now had to be made up. In different ways, states stepped in and paid soldiers either in new certificates or in cash.[146]

In sum, the bulk of the public debt had been depreciated or paid off or substituted for by 1783. When the impost failed by 1786, states stepped in to assume their share of the debt, leaving only interest here and there and loan certificates to be redeemed.[147] One could say either that Congress and the states separately and together had put together a patchwork of expedients that retired most of the debt, or that the government of the Articles had failed to retire the entire debt in a systematic manner. In any event, insofar as we can discover, a crisis did not exist. Yet, if it is a crisis of perceptions we are talking about, then a significant element of American political elites decided there was a crisis that could be resolved only by what they had believed was necessary all along, namely, a stronger national government.

Whereas von Holst spoke of "the contemptible impotence of Congress,"[148] David Humphreys wrote to Jefferson in 1786 that "to judge by the face of the country; by the appearance of ease and plenty which are to be seen everywhere, one would believe a great portion of the poverty and evils complained of, must be imaginary."[149]

The vital fact, not less vital for being obvious, was that the American states (though they might have behaved, as some said, as if they were in a state of nature toward each other) did not in fact go to war and had no expectation of doing so. What one might say today of the relationships among Western industrial and democratic nations—that they may struggle hard economically but they will not invade or threaten each other's sovereignty[150]—was true then as well. Though it runs counter to conventional understanding, Onuf's explanation goes in the right direction:

> But it was easy to exaggerate the impact of popular discontent and to impute it to "imbecile" government. The success of the American state system—in avoiding interstate warfare and in containing popular discontent—was less conspicuous, because it defied conventional logic. Defects in state power were integral to this success. The combination of limited state power, a general acceptance of a congressional jurisdiction that was rarely invoked, and the actual resolution of disputes by continuing negotiations between or among states and between states and their citizens guaranteed the survival of the American state system.[151]

It is not only the presence but the absence of coercive authority that may prove useful. States could not do much about the acts of other states, and the Congress lacked the ability to force states into line. This was as true for states' inability to coerce settlers in the outlying areas of their territories as it was for their inability to force compliance with their wishes on other states. Since they would not go to war, they were obliged to wheedle, cajole, and bargain, all of which led to more acceptable outcomes than the coercive alternative.[152] "What is truly remarkable about the Confederation," I agree with Wood, "is the degree of union that was achieved."[153]

The Constitution

Much ink has been spilled over the Framers' construction of human nature as sufficiently virtuous to permit republican government but sufficiently immoral to demand controls over insuperable egoism. Too much ink. For if human nature had a tendency toward evil, then it was not possible to trust the people's representatives or, for that matter, the people themselves. How then was government, any government, to be trusted? The nationalists' problem was to create a government that had independent taxing and regulatory powers. The barrier to this effort had been the belief that the states were sovereign and that, therefore, the liberty of the people depended on requiring that any national entity exercise its power through and not apart from the states.

But if state governments were also tainted with the inherent corruption of human nature, the only repository of authority that remained, however suspect it might also be, was the people themselves. How easy it was, in this conception, to argue that representatives not only sought to aggrandise themselves through their inevitable and invariable lust for power, but that they committed the opposite but equally venal sin of giving in to popular passions that extended from common human depravity. Why, then, not put a national government over states to constrain their wickedness, claiming all the while that the separation of powers between executive, legislative, and judicial functions would suffice to limit evils of the national entity? If separation of powers was desirable so as to limit the evils of human egoism, why not go a step further and divide the powers in some sense between national and state entities, thus reducing the capacity for self-aggrandisement even further? Thus a national government became the answer to two problems at once—not only the lack of a strong central government but also a barrier against real and alleged harms perpetrated by the self-same, self-aggrandizing state legislatures that had thwarted royal governors. Republican ideology served well in opposition, but without a strong executive to counter, it disintegrated. No orthodoxy, no heterodoxy.[154] Only the existence of a national executive under the Constitution revived their political fortunes.

Hoisted by their own petard! Historians have pointed out that the anti-federalists were poorly organized and did not appear to be very good politicians. Though some were concerned that the Annapolis convention of September 1786, formed explicitly to revise the Articles of Confederation, might undermine state sovereignty, they had no alternative to offer. As the South Carolina anti-federalist, Aedanus Burke put it, "We had no principle of concert or union."[155] The concerns of the anti-federalists lay in state and local politics, not in a national entity that could act outside of state approval they did not want. Their egalitarian rhetoric had become antigovernmental as well. The genius of the Framers consisted in turning republican rhetoric upside down. Suddenly, the great beast, as Hamilton once called the populace, became the source of sovereignty investing a national (henceforth called "federal") government with the authority it needed. Of course, state governments were also vested with the same authority but, by the same token, they were created simultaneously with the national government so they had no precedence and therefore no preference over it. Just as Madison turned around the argument that liberty could not exist in a large republic by claiming that it could only subsist there, and Hamilton argued that it was lack of sufficient executive power, not a surfeit of it, that endangered liberty, so now the federalists were able to get their way by arguing that, if the people had sovereignty, they could create simultaneously state and federal governments.

There is a long line of development in the history of American ideas arguing that the American nation existed prior to the states. Story, in his famous *Commentaries on the Constitution of the United States*, held that the colonies lacked essential attributes of sovereignty while they were ruled by Britain, so that whatever sovereignty they acquired came from the Declaration of Independence and then the Constitution.[156] This interpretation runs against the evidence presented that states (or colonies) existed prior to the nation. Yet human ingenuity knows few bounds. Essentially, the argument is that the Revolutionary War dissolved the colonies that then became states by virtue either of the Declaration of Independence or of the Continental Congress whose acts enabled them to reformulate themselves somehow as creatures of national government or on the same par with it. Furthermore, picking up hints from the Founding Fathers, theorists argued that the people through state constitutional conventions established

both state and national governments so that they were at least cotermi-
nous in time and authority with one another.[157]

In our time, Curtis Nettels held that Congress, "the United Colonies," was sovereign because the colonies existed before states were
formally created. These states might have been free when controlled
by Britain, but they were formed by the American Union.[158] This view
has been taken up by historian Richard B. Morris, to whom "the
historical evidence indicates that a national government was in operation before the formation of the states. It was the people who initiated
the holding of the First Continental Congress, delegates to which were
selected in disregard of the colonial assemblies and by other extralegal
means, and issued the call for the Second Congress."[159] Morris further
claims that "The colonies accepted the initiative of Congress, as well
as its authority, in their transformation into thirteen states exercising
only internal sovereignty."[160] Those who disagree Morris calls "intractable states-righters."[161] I have argued that this view is mistaken.

One might claim that sovereignty resided in the ratifying conventions, popularly elected, who had the power to reject the Constitution.
The argument would be that these conventions were not state governments but reflections of popular will, hence sovereignty remained with
the people. But the conventions were created by the state legislatures.
When one looks at the resolutions of the General Assembly of Virginia on October 16, 1786 ("deputies . . . devising and discussing all
such Alterations and further Provisions as may be necessary to render
the Federal Constitution adequate") and the Delaware resolution of
February 3, 1787 by its General Assembly ("deputies deliberating on,
and discussing, such Alterations and further Provisions") the die was
cast for more than mere revision of the Articles of Confederation.

"Where did sovereignty go," Forrest McDonald asked, when George
III "abdicated" it? One answer was that it reverted to the states. Another was that sovereignty passed to Congress under the Articles. Those
who wished to place sovereignty in a national government and that
government alone, like George Reed and Alexander Hamilton, soon
realized they could not get away with it. So they proposed instead that
the national government be given vetos over state legislation. John
Dickinson came up with the nationalist solution: one branch of the
legislature, elected directly by the people, and another, representing
the states (in those days, state legislatures would choose senators).[162]

What, for these aristocratic men, could be more popular than that? When the Framers decided to submit the Constitution not to the state legislatures but to state conventions, they created a national government along side of and in some respects superior to state governments.

American Political Cultures

A little political culture analysis will take us a long way. Colonial America fought the war against a distant hierarchy exemplified by King George III. The economy of Great Britain was mercantilist, which, for our purpose, means hierarchically organized. Though feudalism had passed, society was still highly stratified into clearly defined higher and lower strata. Though Parliament could be powerful—were it unified—it most often was not. In the middle of the eighteenth century, factions within the top levels of society competed for control of British government. In short, Great Britain could be described largely as a hierarchical society with rising but by no means dominant individualism.

The colonists, by contrast, contained adherents of three political cultures. With over 90 percent of the populace made up of small farmers, it is not surprising that most Americans were competitive individualists. Their question was whether markets were free or rigged by those with governmental connections. Adherents of hierarchical culture were divided between loyalists (many of whom fled to Canada) and nationalists who sought fortune and fame at home. Then there were egalitarians imbued with republican spirit who sought to reduce differences (they would have said "privileges") of all kinds. Like Jefferson, they believed that representative government was possible in the United States, given its vast resources, provided that the national government did not confer favors (corruption, they called it) on some not available to others—debt, franchises, government banks, patronage.[163] Egalitarians like Sam Adams were in the forefront of the Revolution. With these three orienting dispositions set out, we can begin to make sense of government in America before and after the Revolution.

The war on the American side was fought by a multicultural coalition—individualists and egalitarians opposed the restrictions imposed by the British monarchy. American hierarchists wished those entitled to rule in their own country, people like themselves, to take the place of their British counterparts.

With the war won, hierarchy in disrepute, and many hierarchists in Canada, the nationalists were unable to get a government to their liking. Even the modest form of national government in the Dickinson draft of the Articles was decisively defeated. For a time the running was with egalitarians and individualists who agreed to keep central government small. For egalitarians this meant protection against the corruption of privilege; for individualists, a weak central government meant fewer regulations and lower taxes.

But then hierarchical nationalists became outraged by signs of anarchy. It was not only attacks on private property, pro-debtor policies, and interference with free trade; nationalists also objected to what seemed to them a denigration of the status of all Americans when there was no political hierarchy to speak for them as a nation.

Alone, however, the hierarchical nationalists could not succeed. Though they were brilliant propagandists, they could not have succeeded without support from a section of individualists, preeminently merchants and landowners concerned about facilitating trade and protecting private property. No doubt individualists were divided by state boundaries and economic interests. And that is the point: their previous solidarity against the hierarchical system of the British began to give way to concern about insufficient national power to protect property and trade. Signs of rebellion and restraint of trade led individualists to fear they might lose all for lack of even a minimal state. Thus the individualist alliance against hierarchy became a coalition of individualists and hierarchists against egalitarianism in the form of too democratic state legislatures. Nor could the nationalists have been as successful as they were without the aforementioned weakness of the anti-federalists. Unable to act to strengthen the Articles, because even mild changes might be too much, their characteristic denigration of all forms of authority prevented them from constructing their own forms or realizing that, in the Articles, they already had it.

What If . . .

At the time, no one could have imagined the growth of national power. The size and scope of government today would then literally have been unimaginable. States still matter because government has grown at all levels, but there is no doubt that the federal government has grown comparatively greater. Could this development have been deterred? Would there have been a different development had the Articles of Confederation remained in force?

I realize that, for some, the Constitution has assumed the status of a holy object. No disparagement is intended. My purpose is to reclaim partially some lost knowledge of what might have been had these United States of America done what it came within a whisker of doing—living under a noncentralized system of government.

One difficulty is that while we know a great deal (or at least something) about how things turned out under American federalism, we know nothing about how a noncentralized system would have worked, except for the scant few years under the Articles. What have we learned?

Noncentralized systems take a while to get organized. Different elements sometimes move in different ways. But they begin to see advantages in cooperation, first on a basis of bilateral bargaining, then in larger circles of mutual advantage. Whether we are talking about retaliatory tariffs or interferences with commerce or wartime debts, the trend is toward larger realms of cooperation. Without putting down any state (unless, as in Shay's Rebellion, it was a state of lawlessness), the cession of land by New York and Massachusetts, together with the sequence of events leading up to the Northwest Ordinance, set upon the path of solution the one problem—disposition of the western lands—that could have prevented American expansion into the lower half of the North American continent.

Had there not been a unanimity requirement for amendments to the Articles, the impost would have passed. But, as we saw, there is no reason to believe that under the wartime circumstances any national government could have collected the revenue. And there is every reason to believe that the purpose of Alexander Hamilton's federal assumption of state debt—firmly to establish federal credit—was well on its way to achievement by the time he took office.

The struggle over federal assumption, which Jefferson said was the most fierce of his long lifetime, raised the question of equality and privilege in a pronounced form. Much debt had been bought up from veterans by speculators who stood to gain enormously. Hamilton presented the issue as one of getting all concerned, at home and abroad, to know that the federal government was a reliable payer. To Americans with an egalitarian-republican worldview, however, everything they hated was summed up in their belief, not entirely unfounded, that federal assumption was not only or mainly about credit but about attaching men of means to the federal government as a replacement for the foreign hierarchy they had recently overthrown. Without much if any loss to national credit, the noncentralized Articles might have avoided this bitter struggle altogether. And the national capital might not have been established in a pestilential swamp.

With less fear of a too-powerful national government, the nation might have been better prepared for the War of 1812. In any event, it could hardly have been worse prepared than it was under the federal government.

The struggles over the establishment of a national bank might well have been avoided under the Articles. The requirement of state consent would have rendered a national bank unfeasible. Instead of today's fiat currency, there would likely have been competing currencies. Over time, the sounder currency would have spread over the country, a currency kept sounder by the threat of rival currencies.

One of the most impressive arguments against remaining with the Articles of Confederation was the widespread belief that it lacked the central power to prohibit endless issues of paper money in favor of debtors, thus inflating the currency. That, in a different guise, is exactly what happened under the Constitution. Did not the Constitution explicitly state that only the national government could issue currency? Yes, it did but, no, this provision was not effective as Gordon Wood tells us in his splendid *The Radicalism of the American Revolution*: "People wanted, indeed needed, paper money, and despite the framers' best intention the people simply pressed their state legislatures to charter banks that in turn issued the paper money that was desired."[164] Though "only" twenty-five banks were established in the period between 1790 and 1800, by 1820 there were over 300 state banks. Governors vetoed the establishments; legislatures commonly overrode them. True, these were merely bank notes, yet, nevertheless, they passed as money considering that they promised to pay in gold or silver.[165] Had the identical series of developments occurred under the Articles of Confederation, this phenomena would undoubtedly have been charged to the weakness of its central government.

The Civil War must remain problematic. On the one hand, efforts in the South to nullify federal laws might have been more successful. On the other hand, there might have been less need to attempt nullification because the desires of the Southern states would have had to be taken into account in a more pronounced way.

These preliminaries open up the necessarily inconclusive question of whether slavery might have lasted longer under a non-centralized system. Maybe not. Had the Southern states seceded from the Confederation, there then might have been much the same struggle over whether the new states formed out of the territories would be slave or free. Maybe yes. Who can say whether a more protracted period of slavery, leading sooner rather than later to the abolition of slavery by the Southern states (which, in an increasingly industrial society we may treat as a near certainty), would have been better or worse for the former slaves? There is the chance that a less coerced abolition, done in the same of Southern self-interest, might have spared the nation something of the legacy of racism.

The Civil War exerted a powerful nationalizing effect. Before Abraham Lincoln's assassination, he had completed virtually the entire nationalization program of his political hero, Henry Clay, the leader of the Whig party, which succeeded Hamilton's hierarchical Federalist (better called nationalist) party. If we remember that the Republican party after the Civil War was, for a time, the successor to the Clay, Lincoln, governmental interventionist party of so-called internal improvements, the ratio of national to state government activity might well have been smaller. Indeed, slavery, therefore race and civil war are closely tied. Unequal outcomes by race are even today cited as rationales for expanding governmental welfare programs.

Might the United States have avoided its occupation of the Philippines and the conquest of Cuba under a noncentralized system? If jingoism was spread equally throughout the country, nothing would have been different. If not, not. In general, going to war would have been more difficult under a noncentralized system.

Would the American welfare state have grown as far and as fast as it has? The usual question is why the United States has been a welfare laggard compared to Western Europe. Compared to its own early traditions, however, United States welfare programs are very large and growing larger. Probably the states under the Articles would have differentiated themselves more. In *Protecting Soldiers and Mothers*, Theda Skocpol demonstrates that many states, at the urging of women's groups, adopted pensions for widows and other maternalist programs.[166] What we cannot know is whether pressures for national uniformity would have led states to adopt comparable programs.

Either institutions matter or they don't. It has been argued that the

American federal system, which gives power to states, has delayed and diminished welfare programs.[167] If that is so, then even stronger state power could have been an even more powerful hindrance.

I do not wish further to strain the reader's credulity. The rhetoric of "it might have beens" is notoriously slippery. I merely wish to suggest that the history we Americans have had is not the only history there might have been. There is also the brief history of a non-centralized system we did have and the "might have" history we almost had.

Irony

The ultimate irony is that each and every one of the accusations against the Articles of Confederation that were supposed to lead to the collapse of republican government came true under the Constitution. Soon enough the nation proved unprepared for the War of 1812. States under the Constitution defaulted on bonds so often they became objects of ridicule abroad.[168] State-chartered banks issued large amounts of what became, in effect, paper money. Efforts to depreciate the currency continued, and, of course, the Union was put in danger during the Civil War. From this we may well conclude that the faults complained of were part of the growing pains of a young republic likely to have occurred under whatever form of self-government was adopted. The difference is this: as time passed and the act of revolution became enshrined in golden memory, the form of government mistakenly identified with the revolution by transference—the Constitution—gained the legitimacy necessary to overcome the vicissitudes that face every people and nation.

Appendix: Money in Early America[169]

In the fifty to one hundred years after the first settlers arrived during the latter 1600s and early 1700s, there was no money. The first colonists were poor; gold and silver had not yet been discovered. The only currency in circulation was a motley mixture of Dutch, English, and later, Spanish coins. Prices, particularly in New England, might be specified in guilders, pistoles, pieces of eight, doubloons, rit-dollars, as well as pounds and shillings. Each colony valued the separate sets of coins differently, running the metal back and forth, as it were, so one kind of coin disappeared in one place to be succeeded for a time in another. Understandably, the shortage of ready cash was a constant theme of financial complaints.

When coins did not suffice, which was most of the time, trade was conducted in barter. Rice and tobacco in the South, and cattle, corn, and furs in New England, were used to pay bills. A college student might pay tuition with a cow or a goat. Lacking a better method, Dutch settlers began to use Indian shell beads, or "Wampampeake" currency, composed of white beads taken from conch shells and the more rare, and hence more valuable, black beads from mussel or clam shells. Taxes, labor, and court judgments were payable in wampum. Inevitably, the ratio of two white to one black shell varied as much as the value of the currency and depreciated even more given charges levied by settlers or Indians that one or the other had dyed white shells black.

In the absence of commercial banks (before the American Revolution there were none), credit was extended and commerce carried on by merchants. Merchants minted silver "pine-tree shillings," deliberately made twenty-two and a half times lighter than the English variety so they would be retained in the colonies rather than shipped abroad. Other merchants acted as agents of exchange or issued letters of credit to Americans traveling abroad. It was a hit-or-miss business. Debt was undesirable because it was considered by many to be a form of immorality; indeed, the debtor laws were so severe that a hapless soul might find himself in prison without the ability to raise ready money for his release. The desire to experiment with various issues of paper money may well have sprung from the understandable need to facilitate trade and to mitigate the sanctions imposed on debtors.

Another form of currency, treasury bills, were issued by colonies in anticipation of tax notes created to pay for wars or for general administration. These notes passed through so many hands and were of such uncertain value that the practice was finally halted in favor of floating loans in advance of tax collections. Dependent as the colonists were on whatever credit they could internally muster, it is understandable that the English Bubble Act of 1719, forbidding bills of credit to be issued first in England and then in America, led by 1751 to considerable opposition.

Shortage of specie was exacerbated by the wars against the French that occurred intermittently between 1730 and 1760. Taxes rose by as much as ten to twenty times their prewar rates, and under the lash of necessity, several colonial legislatures issued "paper money" in the form of bills of credit that bore interest and required repayment in specie. So long as these bills were only a small portion of available currency, they held up, but eventually they depreciated from half to a tenth of their former value.

Under massive popular pressure, many colonies began to issue paper money, much of which not only fluctuated but rapidly depreciated in value as the printing presses ran overtime. In response, moralistic tracts were written that stressed the desirability of limiting the amount of money in circulation as a bar to inflation. One of Benjamin Franklin's earliest papers was on this subject, though the warning was generally not as necessary to pacifist Pennsylvania, where Quakers steadfastly refused to issue paper money to pay for war. Nonetheless, Franklin's support of British restrictions on paper money led to his only electoral defeat.

Notes

1. Jack N. Rakove, *The Beginnings of National Politics: An Interpretive History of the Continental Congress* (New York: Alfred A. Knopf, 1979), p. 19.
2. Peter S. Onuf, *The Origins of the Federal Republic: Jurisdictional Controversies in the United States, 1775–1787* (Philadelphia: University of Pennsylvania Press, 1983), pp. xiv-xv, 23.
3. Jack P. Greene, "The Background of the Articles of Confederation," *Publius: The Journal of Federalism*, vol. 12, no. 4 (Fall 1982): 15–44, at p. 22.
4. Ibid., p. 23.
5. John M. Murrin, "The British and Colonial Background of American Constitutionalism," in Leonard W. Levy and Dennis J. Mahoney, eds., *The Framing and Ratification of the Constitution* (New York: Macmillan Publishing Co., 1987), p. 26.

6. Donald S. Lutz, "The Articles of Confederation as the Background to the Federal Republic," in *Publius: The Journal of Federalism*, vol. 20, no. 1 (Winter 1990): 55–70, at p. 57.

7. Ibid., p. 58.

8. Ibid.

9. Ibid.

10. Murrin, "The British and Colonial Background of American Constitutionalism," pp. 33–34.

11. Robert C. Newbold, *The Albany Congress and Plan of Union, 1754*. Dissertation, University of Notre Dame, 1953, p. 17.

12. Mullin, "The Albany Congress and Colonial Confederation," *Mid-America, An Historical Review*, vol. 72, no. 2 (April/July 1990): 93–105, at pp. 101–102.

13. Bruce E. Johansen, *Forgotten Founders: Benjamin Franklin, the Iroquois and the Rationale for the American Revolution* (Ipswich, Mass.: Gambit Inc., Publishers, 1982), pp. 61–62.

14. See Elizabeth Tooker, "The United States Constitution and the Iroquois League," in James A. Clifton, ed., *The Invented Indian: Cultural Fictions and Government Policies* (New Brunswick, N.J.: Transaction Publishers); Jose Barreiro, ed., *Indian Roots of American Democracy* (Ithaca, N.Y.: Northeast Indian Quarterly, 1988); Donald A. Grinde, Jr., *The Iroquois and the Founding of the American Nation* (San Francisco: Indian Historical Press, 1977); and Daniel K. Richter, "Ordeals of the Longhouse: The Five Nations in Early American History," in D.K. Richter and J.H. Merrell, eds., *Beyond the Covenant Chain: The Iroquois and Their Neighbrors in Indian North America, 1600–1800* (Syracuse, N.Y.: Syracuse University Press, 1987).

15. Newbold, *The Albany Congress and Plan of Union*, pp. 17–18.

16. Lutz, "The Articles of Confederation as the Background to the Federal Republic," pp. 58–59; and *Dictionary of American History*, revised edition, vol. I (New York: Charles Scribner's Sons, 1976), pp. 59–60.

17. Mark Mayo Boatner III, *Encyclopedia of the American Revolution* (New York: David McKay Co., 1976) pp. 15–16.

18. Lutz, "The Articles of Confederation as Background to the Federal Republic," pp. 59–60; and Robert W. Tucker and David C. Hendrickson, *The Fall of the First British Empire—Origins of the War of American Independence* (Baltimore/ London: John Hopkins University Press, 1982), p. 81.

19. Peter S. Onuf, "The First Federal Constitution: The Articles of Confederation," in L. W. Levy and D. J. Mahoney, eds., *The Framing and Ratification of the Constitution*, p. 84.

20. Rakove, *The Beginnings of National Politics*, p. 17.

21. Gordon S. Wood, *The Creation of the American Republic 1776–1787* (Chapel Hill, N.C.: University of North Carolina Press, 1969), p. 356.

22. Onuf, "The Origins of the Federal Republic," p. 27.

23. Yehoshua Areli, *Individualism and Nationalism in American Ideology* (Cambridge, Mass.: Harvard University Press, 1964), p. 33.

24. Ibid.

25. John Adams, quoted in Onuf, "The First Federal Constitution," p. 86.

26. Greene, "The Background of the Articles of Confederation," p. 25.

27. Rakove, *The Beginnings of National Politics*, pp. 81–82, 96; and Wood, *The Creation of the American Republic*, p. 130.

28. Donald S. Lutz, "The First American Constitutions," in L. W. Levy and D. J. Mahoney, eds., *The Framing and Ratification of the Constitution*, pp. 73–74.

29. Ibid., p. 75.
30. Leonard W. Levy, "Introduction: American Constitutional History, 1776–1789," in L.W. Levy and D.J. Mahoney, eds., *The Framing and Ratification of the Constitution*, p. 8.
31. Claude H. Van Tyne, "Sovereignty in the American Revolution: An Historical Study," *American Historical Review*, vol. VII (April 1907): 529–545, at p. 543.
32. Ibid., p. 536.
33. Irving Brant, "A Letter to the Editor," *William and Mary Quarterly*, vol. XV, no. 1, 3rd series (January 1958), p. 137.
34. Edmund S. Morgan, "Colonial Ideas of Parliamentary Power," *William and Mary Quarterly*, vol. V, no. 3, (July 1948): 311–341, at pp. 325–326.
35. Andrew C. McLaughlin, "The Background of American Federalism," *American Political Science Review*, vol. XII, no. 1 (February 1918): 215–240, at pp. 215–219.
36. Quoted in Rakove, *The Beginnings of National Politics*, p. 32.
37. See K. C. Wheare, *Federal Government* (New York/London: Oxford University Press, 1947).
38. I have adopted here the argument of Tucker and Hendrickson in *The Fall of the First British Empire*. The argument is also consistent with my earlier essays in this volume.
39. Charles R. Ritcheson, *British Politics and the American Revolution* (Norman, Okla.: University of Oklahoma Press, 1954), pp. 3–4.
40. Robert W. Tucker and David C. Hendrickson, *The Fall of the First British Empire—Origins of the War of American Independence*, pp. 55–56.
41. Robert Middlekauff, *The Glorious Cause: The American Revolution 1763–1789* (New York/Oxford: Oxford University Press, 1982), p. 57.
42. Ritcheson, *British Politics and the American Revolution*, pp. 100–101.
43. Ibid., pp. 218–219.
44. Tucker and Hendrickson, *The Fall of the First British Empire*, pp. 201–202.
45. Ibid., p. 150.
46. Rakove, *The Beginnings of National Politics*, pp. 21–22.
47 Ibid pp 140–141
48. Edmund Cody Burnett, *The Continental Congress* (New York: The Macmillan Company, 1941), p. 35.
49. Van Tyne, "Sovereignty in the American Revolution," pp. 530–533.
50. Ibid., p. 45.
51. Greene, "Background of the Articles of Confederation," pp. 15–16.
52. Burnett, *The Continental Congress*, pp. 1–60 inter alia.
53. Rakove, *The Beginnings of National Politics*, pp. 78–79.
54. Joseph L. Davis, *Sectionalism in American Politics* (Madison: University of Wisconsin Press, 1977), pp. 10–11.
55. Calvin C. Jillson, "Political Culture and the Pattern of Congressional Politics under the Articles of Confederation," *Publius* (Winter 1988): 1–26, at p. 25.
56. Ibid., pp. 25–26.
57. Rakove, *The Beginnings of National Politics*, p. 283–284.
58. Jillson, "Political Culture and the Pattern of Congressional Politics under the Articles of Confederation," pp. 13–14.
59. Middlekauff, *The Glorious Cause*, pp. 515–516.
60. Ibid., p. 514.
61. Ibid., pp. 516–517.

62. Ibid., pp. 517–518.
63. Ibid., p. 518.
64. Rakove, *The Beginnings of National Politics*, p. 166.
65. Ibid., pp. 165–166.
66. Ibid., pp. 206–207.
67. Tucker and Hendrickson, *The Fall of the First British Empire*, pp. 101–102. A statement by Robert Morris, the financier who tried to put finances on a better footing, will help set the stage: "But what else could be expected from us? A Revolution, a War, the Dissolution of Government, the creating of it anew, Cruelty, Rapine and Devastation in the midst of our very Bowels, these Sir are Circumstances by no means favorable to Finance. The wonder then is that we have done so much, that we have borne so much, and the candid World will add that we have dared so much" (quoted in Rakove, *The Beginnings of National Politics*, p. 292).
68. Leonard W. Levy, "Introduction: American Constitutional History, 1776–1789," p. 7.
69. Rakove, *The Beginnings of National Politics*, p. 282.
70. Ibid., p. 7.
71. Rakove, *The Beginnings of National Politics*, pp. 282–283.
72. Levy, "Introduction: American Constitutional History," pp. 207–208.
73. Jackson Turner Mann, *The Antifederalists: Critics of the Constitution* (Chapel Hill, N.C.: University of North Carolina Press, 1961), p. 84.
74. Jillson, "Political Culture and the Pattern of Congressional Politics," p. 18.
75. Rakove, *The Beginnings of National Politics*, p. 340–341.
76. Middlekauff, *The Glorious Cause*, pp. 584–85.
77. Piers Mackesy, *The War for America* (London: Longmans, Green & Co., 1964), pp. xiv, 5.
78. Middlekauff, *The Glorious Cause*, p. 576.
79. Mackesy, *The War for America*, p. 23.
80. Ibid., pp. 2–6.
81. R. Arthur Bowler, *Logistics and the Failure of the British Army in America 1775–1783* (Princeton, N.J.: Princeton University Press, 1975), pp. 247–253. Now I understand better the Jane Austen novels in which, whatever the merits of the deserving young man he does not advance without a patron.
82. Ibid., pp. 248–249; Mackesy, *The War for America*, pp. 13, xv.
83. Bowler, *Logistics and the Failure of the British Army in America*, pp. 249–56.
84. Ibid., pp. 256–257.
85. Quoted in ibid., pp. 246–247.
86. Quoted in ibid., p. 246.
87. Ibid., p. 241.
88. Mackesy, *The War for America*, p. 63.
89. Bowler, *Logistics and the Failure of the British Army in America*, p. 231.
90. Ibid., pp. 229–230.
91. Ibid., p. 228.
92. Ibid., pp. 228–229.
93. Middlekauff, *The Glorious Cause*, p. 512.
94. Though one could hardly call the Whig opposition "pro-American," Ritcheson tells us, "Yet the Americans and the Opposition shared much common ground: a belief that King and ministers had somehow—mysteriously though corruptly—come to dominate the political scene free of any constitutional check. Both

groups detected in the reign of George III an insidious attempt to re-create old Stuart despotism" (Ritcheson, *British Politics and the American Revolution*, pp. 217–218).

95. Wood, *The Creation of the American Republic*, p. 70.
96. Mann, *The Antifederalists*, pp. 10–11. See also Aaron Wildavsky, *The Rise of Radical Egalitarianism* (Washington, D.C.: American University Press, 1991), ch. 2, "Resolved, That Individualism and Egalitarianism Be Made Compatible in America: Political Cultural Roots of Exceptionalism," and ch. 3, "The Internal Transformation of the Major Political Parties: Democratic Activists Are Increasingly Egalitarian, Republicans Individualist and Hierarchical."
97. Ibid., p. 10.
98. Quoted in ibid., pp. 108–109. See also Wood, *The Creation of the American Republic*, p. 399.
99. Wood, *The Creation of the American Republic*, p. 400.
100. Middlekauff, *The Glorious Cause*, p. 47.
101. Wood, *The Creation of the American Republic*, p. 135.
102. Lance Banning, *The Jeffersonian Persuasion, Evolution of a Party Ideology* (Ithaca/London: Cornell University Press, 1978), p. 85.
103. Wood, *The Creation of the American Republic*, pp. 353–354.
104. Quoted in ibid., p. 357.
105. See Lutz, "The Articles of Confederation as the Background to the Federal Republic," p. 62.
106. Merrill Jensen, "The Articles of Confederation: A Re-interpretation," *Pacific Historical Review*, vol. VI, no. 2 (June 1937): 120–142, at p. 133.
107. Ibid., p. 142.
108. Michael P. Zuckert, "A System without Precedent: Federalism in the American Constitution," in L.W. Levy and D.J. Mahoney, eds., *The Framing and Ratification of the Constitution*, pp. 136–137.
109. Quoted in "Sovereignty over Seabeds," p. 1062.
110. Quoted in ibid., p. 1063.
111. Rakove, *The Beginnings of National Politics*, pp. 167–168.
112. Ibid., pp. 166–167.
113. Ibid., p. 172.
114. Lutz, "The Articles of Confederation as Background to the Federal Republic," p. 66.
115. Winton U. Solberg, ed., *The Federal Convention and the Formation of the Union of the American States* (New York: The Liberal Arts Press, 1958), p. 43.
116. Ibid., p. 44.
117. Ibid., p. 46.
118. Rakove, *The Beginnings of National Politics*, p. 88a.
119. Ibid., pp. 355–356.
120. James F. Shepherd and Gary M. Walton, "Economic Changes after the American Revolution. Pre- and Post-War Comparisons of Maritime Shipping and Trade," *Explorations in Economic History*, vol. 13, no. 4 (Oct. 1976): 397–422, at pp. 419–420.
121. Gordon C. Bjork, "The Weaning of the American Economy: Independence, Market Changes, and Economic Development," *Journal of Economic History*, vol. XXIV, no. 4 (Dec. 1964): 541–560, at pp. 542–560.
122. Shepherd, *Economic Changes*, pp. 415–419.
123. Ibid., pp. 420–421.

124. Edmund W. Kitch, "Regulation and the American Common Market," in A. Dan Turlock, ed., *Regulation, Federalism, and Interstate Commerce* (Cambridge, Mass.: Oelgeschalger, Gunn & Hain, Inc., 1981), pp. 15–16.

125. William Frank Zornow, "The Tariff Policies of Virgnia, 1775–1789," *The Virginia Magazine of History and Biography*, vol. 62, no. 3 (July 1954): 306–319, at pp. 307–308.

126. Kitch, "Regulation and the American Common Market," p. 17.

127. Ibid., pp. 17–18.

128. Ibid., p. 19.

129. Zornow, "The Tariff Policies of Virginia," p. 313.

130. Ibid., p. 350.

131. Ibid., pp. 315–316.

132. William Frank Zornow, "Massachusetts Tariff Policies, 1775–1789," *The Essex Institute Historical Collections*, vol. XC (April 1954): 194–216.

133. William Frank Zornow, "Tariff Policies in South Carolina, 1775–1789," *The South Carolina Historical Magazine*, vol. 56, no. 1 (January 1955): 31–44, at pp. 37–39.

134. Ibid., pp. 39–43. See also Charles Gregg Singer, *South Carolina in the Confederation*, dissertation from the University of Pennsylvania (Philadelphia, 1941).

135. Richard B. Morris, "The Confederation Period and the American Historian," *William and Mary Quarterly*, vol. XIII, no. 2 (April 1956): 139–156, at p. 140.

136. Richard D. Brown, "Shay's Rebellion and the Ratification of the Federal Constitution in Massachusetts," in Richard Beeman, Stephen Botein, and Edward C. Carter II, eds., *Beyond Confederation—Origins of the Constitution and American National Identity* (Chapel Hill/London: University of North Carolina Press, n.d.), pp. 115–116.

137. Ibid., pp. 117–127.

138. Middlekauff, *The Glorious Cause*, pp. 588–590.

139. Ibid., pp. 588–589.

140. See Aaron Wildavsky, "On the Balance of Budgetary Cultures," in Ralph Clark Chandler, ed., *A Centennial History of the Administrative State* (New York: Macmillan, 1987), pp. 379–413.

141. Mann, *The Antifederalists*, pp. 6–7.

142. E. James Ferguson, "State Assumption of the Federal Debt during the Confederation," *The Mississippi Valley Historical Review*, vol. 38, no. 3 (December 1951): 403–424, at pp. 409–411.

143. Ibid., p. 424.

144. Ibid., p. 405.

145. Ibid., pp. 405–406.

146. Ibid.

147. Ibid., p. 421; and Richard B. Morris, "The Confederation Period and the American Historian," *William and Mary Quarterly*, vol. XIII, no. 2, 3rd series (April 1956): 139–156, at pp. 151–152.

148. Ibid., p. 144.

149. Wood, *The Creation of the American Republic*, p. 395.

150. See Max Singer and Aaron Wildavsky, *The Real World Order. Zones of Peace/ Zones of Turmoil* (Chatham, N.J.: Chatham House, 1993).

151. Onuf, *The Origins of the Federal Republic*, p. 6.

152. See ibid., pp. 11–12.

153. Wood, *The Creation of the American Republic*, p. 359.

154. See the chapters on egalitarians in Mary Douglas and Aaron Wildavsky, *Risk*

and Culture: An Essay on the Selection of Technological and Environmental
Dangers (Los Angeles/Berkeley: University of California Press, 1982).

155. Wood, *The Creation of the American Republic*, pp. 485–486.
156. 3rd edition, 1958, p. 138.
157. N. Dane, "A General Abridgement and Digest of American Law," no. 11 (1829).
158. Curtis P. Nettels, *The Origin of the Union and of the States*, 72 Proceedings of the Massachusetts Historical Society, vol. 68 (1957–60).
159. Richard B. Morris, "The Forging of the Union Reconsidered: A Historical Refutation of State Sovereignty over Seabeds," *Columbia Law Review*, vol. 74 (October 1974), 6: 1068.
160. Ibid., p. 1071.
161. Ibid.
162. Forrest McDonald, *Novus Ordo Seclorum: The Intellectual Origins of the Constitution* (Lawrence: University Press of Kansas, 1985), pp. 147–150, 214–215.
163. See Aaron Wildavsky, "Resolved, that Individualism and Egalitarianism Be Made Compatible in America: Political-Cultural Roots of Exceptionalism," in Byron E. Shafer, ed., *Is America Different? A New Look at American Exceptionalism* (Oxford/New York: Oxford University Press, 1991).
164. Gordon Wood, *The Radicalism of the American Revolution* (New York: Alfred A. Knopf, 1992), p. 316.
165. Ibid., pp. 316–317.
166. Aaron Wildavsky, review of Theda Skopcol, *Protecting Soldiers and Mothers*, *Journal of Policy History* v. 5, no. 4, (1993), pp. 485–500.
167. Theodore J. Lowi, "Why Is There No Socialism in the United States? A Federal Analysis," in Robert T. Golembiewski and Aaron Wildavsky, eds., *The Costs of Federalism* (New Brunswick, N.J.: Transaction Publishers, 1984), pp. 37–54.
168. Here is a nice bit of doggerel from the Rev. Sidney Smith:
Yankee Doodle borrows cash,
Yankee Doodle spends it,
And then he snaps his fingers at
The jolly flat who lends it.
Ask him when he means to pay,
He shows no hesitation,
But says he'll take the shortest way
And that's Repudiation!
Yankee vows that every State
Is free and independent:
And if they paid each other's debts,
There'd never be an end on't.
They keep distinct till "settling" comes,
And then throughout the nation
They all become "United States"
To preach Repudiation!
And what does freedom mean, if not
To whip our slaves at pleasure
And borrow money when you can,
To pay it at your leisure?
From Aaron Wildavsky, "On the Balance of Budgetary Cultures," in Ralph Clark Chandler, ed., *A Centennial History of the Administrative State* (New York: Macmillan, 1987), pp. 379–413; at pp. 406–407.
169. From ibid., pp. 386–387.

Index